What To Do When It Rains

Rains

A Handbook For Leaders In Crisis

by
Toni Lynn Chinoy

ISBN 1-893652-09-2

Catapult Press
P.O. Box 32113
Hillsboro, VA, 20134
(540) 668-7158

Dedication

to my son David, who is so willing to look at himself as he constantly aspires to perfection in his concept of leadership

Contents

Fundamentals of Leadership

SUMMARY

ACKNOWLEDGEMENTS

To Albrecht von Ziegner, I thank you for the inspiration, ideas, and understanding developed from your work with horses to create the concepts in this book. I wish to express my gratitude to all those patient souls over the years of creating this book, who edited endless copies, who tried and tested the concepts, and who put up with my endless pleas of "Why can't this be finished?" To my editors, Ingrid Lang, Marc Chinoy, Carolyn Blesi, John Anderson, and Leon Krain, and many others who offered their comments, a profound thank you for your energy, effort, and persistence in helping me create a book of which I'm proud. To Jamie Kalvestran, I thank you for your creativity and professionalism in designing the cover for this work, as well as the many other successful projects we have done together. I also wish to acknowledge Sara Huntington as the exceptionally professional photographer who works intensely to create the work that will please the eye of the most critical of all people, her customers.

PREFACE

You've been there. You have experienced the feelings of despair and helplessness that rise with every breath you take. You have seen the obstacles that build one at a time to torpedo your hope. You have felt the drain of energy consumed with every sandbag you throw in front of the rising water. There is a continual battle with your emotions to ignore the fear. It is a constant effort to keep moving, to keep deciding, to carry on ahead of the tidal wave that never recedes, never lets up. There is the courage you always find somewhere in your reservoir that makes you proud, even as you wonder if the pressure will ever end. The questions you do not want to examine: "How long can I keep doing this? Do others know how tired I am? Does it show? Can others tell how out of control I feel?"

Being in control of events affecting your life and your areas of responsibility is a form of mastery. Being in control during stressful times is the act of a master. Whether you choose mastery consciously, or not, is irrelevant. If you are in a position of leadership or responsibility, you have an obligation to attempt to be in control. Unfortunately, your training may not have adequately prepared you for the times.

Performance does not happen by accident. Consistently extraordinary performance is developed over time and is only created by incredible attention to detail. The professional athlete offers a good example. Somewhere in his or her background is a trainer who understood the fundamentals of the sport and had the ability to communicate them to the talented pupil. Through constant practice and testing, the professional athlete learns to perform at peak no matter what the circumstance. He or she relies on an understanding of the basics of his or her sport in tough situations.

1

To develop the appropriate training for leadership, leadership must be broken into its most fundamental components. Next, an understanding of the components and how they fit together to create a composite picture of the most powerful of individuals must be developed.

In determining the fundamental elements of leadership development, it is helpful to explore an example. There is a relatively little known equestrian sport called Dressage. Dressage is a form of horsemanship originally conceived as a methodology for training high-performance horses for war. In the thick of battle the horse must perform with a consistency and power, ultimately acting as a piece of weaponry.

To train this high-performance horse, there is a specific starting place, and a sequence of key steps that are developed patiently over a period of time. Mastery, true mastery, can not be rushed. The first and most important step in a training program is always *relaxation*. The trainer must be committed to the long-term objective of a horse in perfect control under any circumstance. The horse's very basic understanding of relaxed, fluid movement is the only logical starting place. No horse will sustain high performance, particularly in high-stress situations, if the animal has learned to be tense or fearful.

One after another, each step of preparation for the higher levels is developed in sequence. After developing relaxation, the trainer must develop rhythm in the animal's stride as well as mental state. If the horse is erratic or choppy in its movements, it will never be able to perform the more complex movements required later. As the horse achieves what is called the upper levels, often it will have difficulty with one or more of the movements if the foundation is not correct. The solution is usually to return to the basics and drill until the horse is ready to execute the more complicated maneuver.

The best trainers of horses know what it takes to build the horse from the ground up, focusing on each developmental stage with the same intensity as they later focus on the specific movements the horse must execute flawlessly and precisely. The dancing in place, the rhythmic crossing of the legs to travel to new positions, the instantaneous response to the rider's legs and the precise and perfect execution of all manner of natural and unnatural movements are all a part of the sport.

Mastery of the requirements of dressage, as well as mastery of any highly skilled endeavor, is elusive. Few horses achieve it. Many so called 'trainers' do not know or understand the sequencing of steps and the affect of the sequence on the outcome. There are many who assume the title of trainer who are never able to create the desired outcome. Why should mastery of any concept be different?

The premise of *What To Do When It Rains* is that if you know the fundamental elements of successful decision-making for leadership and about life, your process for responding to and thinking about the challenges and crisis will be more powerful and more mature than if you do not. You will learn to return to these fundamentals when all other solutions elude you. If you are striving for a form of mastery, labeling the fundamentals will support you in your journey.

The concepts and fundamentals outlined in this text were developed from studying the dynamics of both successful and not so successful individuals and organizations. The horse trainer, the master teacher of mathematics, and the golf pro have something in common. They all understand the building blocks of their area of expertise. Similar to the perspective gained when dividing a substance into its molecular components, a person can learn to build and reconstruct reality with an understanding of the fundamental components of powerful leadership and decision-making.

What To Do When It Rains defines a set of arbitrary fundamental components for strong and powerful leadership in all circumstances.

The fundamentals offered here follow a natural and logical progression of skill development for a leader. They also apply to many other areas of expertise. As you read, apply the fundamentals to your sport or your life and determine the relevance for you.

What To Do When It Rains was originally written for individuals with huge levels of responsibility, desperate for content that would help them cope with the enormous stresses of their lives. The concepts, however, work for anyone, leader or not, crisis or good times.

The text breaks the development of mastery into three phases. Each phase is a stage in the evolution of the strong and effective human being. The first phase deals with a person's ability to manage *fear*. The second phase works with a person's capacity to manage *confusion*. The last phase evolves the individual's capacity to manage *arrogance*. In each of the components within the phases, the reader addresses his or her own abilities, as well as an understanding of the fears, confusions, and arrogance of others.

Each step is critical. If even one of the fundamental steps is missing in the development, the individual will flounder at crucial moments. As you become aware of the role the fundamentals play in execution of decisions, it is probable you will recognize the missing fundamentals in others. The challenge is to recognize the subtle or, sometimes, dramatic influence they have over your own results. Like the horse, the person must return to basics to correct his or her course when the movements become too complex for clarity.

THE FORMAT

What To Do When It Rains uses both an intellectual development of the fundamentals and the parable of a manufacturing company, the Sorot Corporation, named for its founder, to create a simulation of the mental states and obstacles to handling a crisis or crises in real life situations. The story illustrates a series of real events woven together to portray the use of the Fundamentals in crisis. The story is, as you will see, highly focused on a manufacturing setting, but the fundamentals will work regardless of the perspective you are looking from. It offers a very poignant view of these fundamentals in use for a person attempting to lead.

In the story of the Sorot Corporation, John, the CEO, personifies the struggle to do the right thing within the noise challenging our sanity. The most difficult dilemma an individual must face is choosing right action while battling the side of our nature that demands security.

Chapter I is an introduction to the story of the Sorot Corporation. In each subsequent chapter, you will find sections titled: The Fundamental, The Story, Symptoms, Lessons Learned by Powerful People, Ask Yourself, Things to Remember.

The story begins with a crisis. The CEO of the Sorot Corporation is in deep trouble and has no idea what to do. Everything he and his staff have done to try to save their business has failed and they are facing the *symbolic* wall.

You will follow as John, the CEO, begins the process of relearning his fundamental responsibility as leader. As he brings focus to the fundamentals outlined in this text, you will observe a multitude of changes in his organization.

These are true stories. They all happened, though not necessarily in the same corporation. The fundamentals work. The story serves as an illustration of what can happen when a leader focuses on the right things.

CHAPTER 1

THE STORY

The Sorot Corporation

The company was slowly but surely losing significant market share. Nothing helped. The profits had eroded until the corporation was spending more than it was earning. Unfortunately, the company was "buying" customers' business through massive incentives. Even when the company did bring in new business, the new business was not profitable. The board and the leadership of the company were discussing filing Chapter 11.

CEO John Dobbs was panicking. He had no answers and there was a board meeting that same afternoon. He was to tell the board what he intended to do about the crisis.

John paced madly in front of his second in command, Jerry Drake. His frizzy hair was flying behind him as he wore a path on the carpet in front of the window. His angular body hunched over as if he ran a race.

"What am I to do?" he asked his subordinate. "I have no answers. I haven't a clue what we can do to change things. Our customers are leaving in droves to go to our competitors. We've tried everything the competition is doing and following their footsteps doesn't work for us. Why does it work for them?"

Jerry was sitting in a contemporary chair that was part of an arrangement in John's office. One leg was crossed comfortably over the other. His leg swung in time with John as he took great strides up and down the large office. "Just tell them you're going to cut jobs and lay off a crowd of people. Tell them you have the whole leadership team focused on cutting costs. They love that stuff!" suggested Jerry. "It worked the last three times."

AI don't know where we can cut any more costs. We're cutting into the bone now. And labor gets more and more difficult to deal with every time. We have negotiations coming up and they're out for blood."

"Just tell the board they need to trust you," suggested Jerry. "After all, what do those guys know about running this business anyway?"

"I can't do that! Are you crazy?"

"The only other thing I can think of is to blame Bob Skipper. He just can't seem to get off the dime and get our sales back where they're supposed to be. This is really his fault. After all, he is the head of sales. If you tell the board you're going to do something about Bob, you could probably shut them up for a while."

John slowed down for a brief moment. He looked at Jerry with a puzzled expression on his face and then resumed his pacing.

"Well?" asked Jerry. "It really is his fault, you know. He gets paid pretty big bucks to run sales. He should assume the position for his responsibility."

"What?" asked John, coming up short.

"I mean, assume responsibility for his position," said Jerry with a grin. "I guess my tongue got ahead of my thoughts."

"If you were Bob, what would you have done differently?" asked John.

Jerry looked at his nails as if he were trying to determine whether they were groomed well enough. Jerry got a weekly manicure and was meticulous about his looks. "Lots of things. I would have caught this a long time ago before the company was in so much trouble. I'd have shown the competition a thing or two. They would never have tackled us again. It's partly Debbie's fault, too. She's supposed to watch the finances of this company. She should have warned us sooner! Maybe we should get rid of her, too. We need a good old-fashioned housecleaning around here. Eliminating some of the dead weight would straighten things out in a hurry. Put the fear of God into everybody. Then you'd see some action, I bet!"

"Debbie did warn us. She drove us crazy with her doom and gloom reports. I think I recall *you* saying it was her job to be pessimistic and we shouldn't get too caught up by her gloomy view," said John. "And I don't want to do a housecleaning. We're all trying hard to do the right thing. We're scared out of our minds. This is big and there's no way out."

"Well, you better do something or *you'll* be the one who's gone. The board members have no mercy when they need to find someone to blame. They have to be able to show the shareholders they're *doing* something."

John felt tighter and tighter. Never, in his 30 years in the industry, had he seen anything like this. They had cut the margins to nothing and still the competition undercut them. With the labor and material costs going up and up, there was nowhere to turn to get more out of the revenues. He was not sleeping at night. There were deep circles under his eyes. He simply was not prepared for this.

"Jerry, get out of here. You're making this worse. I don't want to hear any more talk about finding a scapegoat. I need time to think."

Jerry slowly unfolded himself from the chair. He looked John over, top to bottom, and said, "I'm worried about you, boss. You seem to be taking this personally. And I've noticed you seem to be having a little trouble making decisions these days. Maybe you ought to think about what's next."

"Go!" said John.

Jerry shrugged his shoulders and strolled in his slow

9

relaxed walk to the door, glancing in the mirror along the way. As he reached his hand up to smooth the hair over his forehead he said, "Good luck with the board. You'll need it."

As he left the second office where Jackie, the receptionist, sat, he ran into Ned Piercing, the head of legal. "I'm worried about John," he said.

"Why?" asked Ned, always eager to gain information. "He's just not himself. He seems to be losing his grip with all the pressure," responded Jerry.

"Well, I guess we'd better keep an eye on him," suggested Ned with a strange gleam in his eye. He whistled a tune as he walked back into his office.

John sat at his desk with his head in his hands. Jackie poked her head in. She had overheard the conversation in the hall between Ned and Jerry and she was worried about her boss. As secretaries and executive assistants often do, she had a very good feel for the undercurrents in the organization at any given time.

"Want to talk?" she asked in a quiet voice. John looked at her with appreciation. Her simplicity always amazed him. She was so loyal and courageous. How badly some of his staff underestimated the potential they had right in their front offices to help them solve their problems.

"I sure do. I'm really stuck this time and I don't know where to turn. My leadership staff is in chaos. Everyone is trying to identify the next body so they can climb above the corpse and get their share of the pickings. The organization is in grave danger and everybody seems to be more concerned with their personal agendas than with solving the problems. I don't know where to start and the board ties my hands in terms of resources. I might be able to do something if I had some money to throw at the problem. What would you do, old wise one?" he asked with a grin at the end of his tirade. "All I can do is comment on what I've observed," said Jackie. "I've been with you for 15 years now and we've been through tough times before. I'm not sure what the answers to the problem are, but I do know there are answers. I've never seen you not come up with *something*. But I think there's a big difference in how you come up with them."

"What do you mean?" John asked with an expectant look on his face. Jackie was so good at sorting through all of the fear and chaos and putting her finger on a root issue. He was very anxious to hear what she would say this time, since he was so totally stymied.

"I've seen you come up with absolutely brilliant ideas that didn't cost a thing before. But you were different. I've never seen you this tense. You're so wrapped up in trying to fix things, you can hardly think. When you're at your most powerful, you have a fearlessness about you that's contagious. No one can resist your ideas."

"You know, I think you're on to something," John said thoughtfully. "I'm certainly not in the best frame of mind for leadership right now."

AI think the issue is more than leadership," said Jackie. "You can tell when an organization is healthy and when it's not. I don't think this organization is healthy right now."

"O.K. Say more," John said with a sigh. He knew she was about to tell him the focus for his first steps. He also knew whatever she suggested was going to be hard work. He was not sure he had the energy left for what was about to come.

Jackie pointed out the obvious. The capacity for leadership was the first thing she focused on. She talked about the divisiveness in the team and the problems with each of the players. None of what she said was new to John. He realized quick fixes were not going to solve the problem. He would still have a leadership problem and an unhealthy organization. All of their quick fixes had led to more chaos. They had continued to make longer term problems for themselves by cutting into the very fabric of their business. He decided to focus on leadership as the most compelling step; first his own, and then the leadership of his team. He needed to know where to start, and Jackie had given him the first clue with her description of his state of tension.

PHASE 1

PREPARATION

MANAGING FEAR

PREPARATION

Phase I constitutes a starting place for focusing your energy when things go wrong. The content within this phase suggests a foundation for all decision-making. The fundamentals within this phase (*Relaxation, Rhythm, and Freedom*) are the beginnings of good decisions. When your decisions are not working, a common trap is to make the situation worse by floundering and making more bad decisions on top of bad decisions. Often, the only way you know this is happening is because the world keeps getting more and more out of control.

The text offers a context for examining yourself as you make the decisions, rather than diagnosing the decisions themselves. Ultimately, you might think of this section as the one which helps you manage fear, both your own and the fears of the people you seek to influence.

CHAPTER II

RELAXATION

Many average people achieve status. Few are truly able to enjoy their position or, if they are in a leadership role, govern well, if they are unable to control their state of tension. When a person is making decisions from a position of tension or fear, the decisions are not of the quality this same person would make in a relaxed state. Relaxation is a fundamental ingredient of strong leadership.

In this scenario, John begins to discover the difference relaxation makes in his approach to the crisis.

THE STORY

John decided to take a walk before the board meeting. This was not his typical behavior. Usually, he was examining documents and preparing financial reports up to the last possible moment. But he knew he was in no shape to meet the probing questions. All of the reports in the world were not going to stop him from hyperventilating.

He drove to his favorite forest preserve five miles from the office. The day was bitter cold, but John did not mind. As he stepped out of the car, he found himself taking great gulping breaths of air.

"My God," he thought, "I don't remember the last time I really took a deep breath." He began to feel better in moments. He took off at a brisk walk down the path. The

15

ground was hard and the air was clear. He did not even try to think for the first fifteen minutes. He felt numb.

Finally, he began to grapple with his approach to the board. "What am I so afraid of?" he wondered out loud. "Am I afraid I'll lose my job?" As he examined what losing his job would mean, he realized, at some level, losing his job was part of what he was dreading. He had a big mortgage and two kids in college; certainly some heavy responsibility.

"So, if I lost my job, what would I do?" he wondered. He had found, over his life, examining worst outcomes was often helpful. He processed how he would cope, how many reserves he had, how long he could hold out and just what might need to be sacrificed. The sorting was not a fun process, but he felt liberated as he thought through his options.

"So I now have a plan," he thought. "What's still bothering me?" An image flitted through his mind. He saw himself explaining to people why he had been asked to resign. What would he say? How would he explain it?

"I'm afraid of failure!" he realized. "I'm afraid if I can't make this work, my whole life has been a waste. And, what would I do next time? The problems won't be any easier in any other corporation these days. I still wouldn't know how to solve a crisis like the one I'm in now." He found himself gulping for air again. His heart was pounding as he identified the real source of his fear.

He was frozen. He knew he would have to turn back soon, but he was no closer to the answers. What would he tell the board?

For five minutes he continued to wrestle with his dilemma. Suddenly, he realized he had always done the best he could. He had always worried about the results. He had never allowed himself the pleasure of enjoying his successes. He spent several moments reviewing mentally the things he had done right over his career.

"I've done a lot of things right," he said to the trees. "This crisis doesn't undo those! The choices I've made took a lot of guts. I've still got guts, even if I don't have answers!" At once, he could feel something let go inside of him. The release was mind-shaking. AI am not a failure because I found a problem I couldn't solve. I'm still who I am. I've still done a lot of things right. I need the support of the board, not their criticism right now. I know what I need to do!"

He headed back to the car. He was going to ask the board for their ideas. He would turn this board meeting into a problem-solving meeting rather than an inquisition. As he thought about the experience and the talent on the board of directors, he wondered why he had not thought of using the board earlier. He realized he had put himself in the position of always needing to have the answers in order not to appear a failure. What an incredible waste of their talent and his energy! God, breathing felt good.

THE FUNDAMENTAL

Relaxation

John discovered something key to his own success. Relaxation as a starting place for high performance is not new. Relaxation is a foundation for mastery of all concepts. Imagine an athlete who does not warm up. Imagine mastering one of the Eastern concepts for fighting without learning how to breathe and relax your muscles. Try to imagine the world class chess champion who was never able to conquer fear or tension. Now, try to imagine a great leader who allowed stress and tension to affect and distort

17

his or her decisions.

Your performance is affected by how stressed you are. Recognizing your own stress levels and the impact of stress on the quality of your choices when you are stressed is profound.

The Connection Between Performance and Relaxation

John was not performing at his best. He knew he was not and Jackie reinforced the feeling with her comment about having seen John in difficult situations in previous times. There was a quality to his thinking this time that was different than in the past. The threatening nature of the times was not what was bothering Jackie. She was looking for a missing style or a quality John had brought to other situations.

Examining your moments of peak performance can be very enlightening in learning how to deal with tension. The term "peak performance" represents those moments when everything works. Your moments of peak performance were moments when you were all-powerful and could make no mistakes. Peak performance could happen anytime. Perhaps what comes to mind is an athletic event, or the energy you had on a specific project.

Usually, there is a sense of otherworldliness in those moments when you are at your peak. The question has been asked many times, particularly in the sports world, "Can this be willed?"

An ever-present quality of moments of peak performance is a lack of tension. You are relaxed and not fearful. You feel powerful. You are able to see through all issues to the most appropriate and timely action. Peak performance rarely occurs when everything is in your favor. Peak performance is the act of operating successfully in *adverse* circumstances.

Imagine someone playing basketball during a period of peak performance. If you introduce fear or tension into the picture, you will notice the picture immediately becomes stilted and constrained. Everything tightens up and performance changes. Peak performance and the kind of tension that tightens our muscles and creases our foreheads do not exist at the same moment.

Some athletes will speak of a tension they feel *before* they enter a period of true peak performance. However, when they speak of the actual period of outstanding performance, there is almost a sense of being detached, as if watching a movie.

It is helpful to return to feelings of peak performance frequently for understanding. There is a reason you remember the moment as a time of peak performance. You remember because the moment was *different*. Peak performance represents rare periods when you are able to forget all of your fears and can operate at your most spontaneous and free.

Relaxation is a key ingredient of the picture. Imagine the peak performance picture without a sense of being composed and unruffled. Recognizing relaxation and freedom from tension and fear as integral to your best moments of performance is the first step. You must become aware of how tension is affecting your ability to make decisions.

SYMPTOMS

Take a deep breath. A really deep breath. All the way to your toes. Now, notice the difference to the way you were breathing a few moments ago. The difference represents the amount of tension you carry. Breath is the most obvious symptom of too much tension, or in other words, a lack of relaxation necessary for peak performance.

Other symptoms are reflected in your style. You know what you are like at your best. *Any* deviation from your best performance represents a lack of relaxation. If you are moving too quickly and making mistakes as a result, you probably are affected by a certain amount of tension. Sluggishness can also indicate tension.

The second most obvious symptom of tension is found within the state of your muscles. Tense muscles are an indicator of a tense mind. Flex your arm. Flex it hard, as hard as you can. When you release it, what do you feel? If you have been tense, you should be able to feel yourself relax as you go down your body, one muscle at a time, flexing and releasing.

The reactions of others to you will also tell you an enormous amount about the tension you may be carrying. Do people become more calm or less calm when you arrive? Do they tighten up in your presence?

The responses of others to you will reveal considerable information. Identify their symptoms of stress or tension. You are responsible for knowing how *you* are affecting those you influence. A good leader prefers others relaxed. When others are relaxed and free from tension *they* are at their best. A powerful person has the ability to create a sense of calm simply by entering a room. Your personal presence should align people rather than create tension in them.

Do you worry? Worry is a symptom. Worry is the antithesis of relaxed and flowing. Anxiety cramps the mind's ability to solve problems.

Inability to focus represents a form of tension. Are you often distracted by other things when you need to focus? Can you shut out other issues when you need to? Or do you bring them with you? Do they affect your performance?

Watch your emotions. Do you anger quickly? Do your reactions to annoyances exceed the real impact of the aggravation?

Do you appear to others to be running continuously? Powerful individuals never appear to be exerting tremendous energy. They may move rapidly, and they may accomplish a great deal. They do not appear to be doing so at the expense of their health or the balance in their lives. Their movements have the appearance of being effortless.

Is your sense of humor easily accessible? Do you quickly find the humor in situations others might obsess over? The loss of our humor is one of the first things to happen when we are tense. Humor is also the quality most useful in reducing tension in others.

Know yourself. Know what your optimum performance level feels like. Know when you are not operating at optimum performance levels. Examining and correcting for tension is the first step to power as a leader.

LESSONS LEARNED BY POWERFUL PEOPLE

The Basic Personality

Each of us possesses a personality style. We make definite statements about who we are with the *way* we make choices and implement them. Some texts describe the style as Type A or Type B personalities. The A personality type indicates a composite picture of a driving, bulldozing, workaholic, while the B personality is laid back, easy going, perhaps even a couch potato.

Often, our personality style becomes the excuse for being driven and obsessive. There are, however, type A personalities who are very relaxed, even as they are decisive or quick. There

21

are B type personalities who move consistently toward their goals even if they are moving in a slow, methodical way.

Whether you are an A or a B type, your behaviors will run along a continuum from effective to ineffective. You possess elements of all the possibilities, with some characteristics being more dominant. Where you are on the continuum may change from moment-to-moment. The challenge is to stay consistently at the most effective end of your range of behavior.

If the person is missing the fundamental attribute of being able to stay relaxed, particularly in tense situations, there are two very important qualities he or she can develop. The first is an understanding of the importance of breathing and the second is an understanding of the importance of beliefs.

A. The Importance of Breathing

Tension can be subtle. You adjust for tension and anxiety as you do for a chronic backache. There are clues to help you intuitively discover the level of stress you are carrying as a result of tension.

The first step to creating a state of relaxation is to understand the impact of breathing. If you stop to think about taking a breath that nourishes every cell in your body, you will begin to get a sense of how shallow your breath is on a moment-to-moment basis. When you are afraid or tense, the first thing you do is stop breathing. Shallowness of breath is evidence of tension. Shallow breath is also detrimental to your overall physical well-being. If you are not nourishing your muscles by breathing appropriately, there is no way you can achieve a condition of relaxation.

If breathing is the first step, then *paying attention to your breathing* is the first step to the first step. Breathing is not something you do once in a while. To achieve a state of consistent relaxation, you must become very disciplined in noticing whether you are even giving your muscles a chance to relax by breathing properly.

Along with breathing, you should have a general sense of what you are like at the highest performance times. What you are ultimately seeking is a *feeling* representative of you at your most powerful.

B. The Importance of Relaxed Muscles

Muscles are key. Breathing can help to relax muscles, but there are other things that can be done as well. Visualization is a wonderful technique for relaxing tense muscles. You can start relaxation by the exercise mentioned under symptoms. Travel down your body flexing and releasing your muscles one at a time.

Next, visualize your body as if you were an x-ray scanner specifically designed to identify tense muscles. Each time you find one holding tension, visualize a pair of hands massaging the muscle until it becomes loose and pliable. Start with the muscles in your head and neck and work down your body.

Another wonderful technique for relaxing muscles has been used to teach riders to relax when they are on the back of a horse. The technique concentrates on your eyes. Make a fist. A really tight fist. Now imagine that your eyes are "soft". Be deliberate. Make your eyes soft. What happens to your fist?

It is almost impossible to hold tension when you are concentrating on making your eyes soft. All of your muscles are forced to become limp if you indeed make your eyes soft. Make up your own visualizations to help you.

C. The Importance of Beliefs

The second most important aspect to reducing the tension inhibiting optimal performance is understanding the impact of beliefs. What you believe to be true about any situation will clearly influence your response. When your belief induces a state of anxiety, you have diminished your potential.

Beliefs are creations of historical perspective. We form beliefs through our experiences and those thinking patterns we have been taught. If beliefs trigger fear or anxiety, they are probably not serving us.

For example, you may have been taught fear or anger can be a source of adrenaline. Perhaps you believe anger gives you a boost of energy when you need it most. The concept of anger producing energy is one of those myths which may be working against you in your desire to maximize your time at high performance levels. In small doses, fear or anger could possibly generate an effective shove. However, as you think about how much time you may be spending in the high anxiety state, you realize you are overworking your system.

Also, tension or anxiety causes reactions based on instinct, rather than on clear and focused thinking. Instinct very often is driven by fear. Frequently, we make our least effective decisions from this state.

The path back to relaxation is one of self-examination. First, you must know when you are responding from a position of anxiety. Your breathing will tell you if the tension is too subtle to recognize otherwise. Second, you must identify the belief creating your stress. Discovering the belief and acknowledging that the belief may be distorting your ability to react powerfully calls for great discipline.

Certain common belief patterns bear examination. For example, the need to *look good* in the eyes of others will often distort performance. Knowing who triggers this need in you is the first step. Examining why is the next.

For each of us, there are certain people who will create in us the symptoms of stress or tension. Breathing changes. Flow changes. Decision-making patterns change. At a subtle level you have beliefs about that person or that position affecting your responses.

Is the person an authority figure? What beliefs do you hold about authority figures? Do you believe they can affect your future? Do you believe you must please certain *types* of people without really understanding why?

Knowing yourself is key. Understanding *why* you are reacting is the most powerful antidote to stressful reactions. Perhaps the person you are reacting to does represent authority. Perhaps he or she *does* hold the key to your future. Your ability to perform to expectations will be greater if you can let go of the anxiety or tension surrounding interactions with this person.

What if he or she really is a bad person? If the worse case is he or she does not appreciate you when you are at your best, perhaps you are making a serious mistake to let such a person control your life. Freeing yourself from the fear and tension surrounding his or her control over your decisions is very important to your overall leadership evolution. Is this individual's opinion worth the loss of your potential?

Examine your beliefs for accuracy. Is your career in jeopardy if you make a mistake? Are you more worried about looking good than *being* good?

Release any beliefs inhibiting your breathing. If you believe your career is the most important thing in your life, you must re-think your belief. Re-frame beliefs causing stress into ones that create relaxation. For example, choose to believe that balance and well-being are more important than career. If the current set of beliefs inhibit your breathing and, therefore, your ability to be at your most powerful, what do you lose by believing balance is more important than pleasing people?

There are two very good reasons for letting go of damaging beliefs. First, each time you identify and let go of a damaging belief, there is a relaxation of a tension which has been with you for a very long time. Damaging beliefs and the tension they create are like the backache. You do not realize how bad you feel until the backache goes away.

Second, finding new belief patterns becomes a way of thinking. Instead of feeling like a victim, you begin to see your interpretation of events as the key to solving problems. The following process will help you begin identifying and letting go of beliefs standing between you and optimum performance. The quality of the release of tension will be determined by how deeply you are willing to explore your thoughts.

Step One: Recognize when you are tense.

Step Two: Adjust and regulate your breathing.

Step Three: Are there similar situations in your past?

Step Four: Identify the belief behind your reactions.

Step Five: Create a new belief for this situation.

This process is effective for the mundane as well as the complex issues in your life. The success of the process depends on the new belief creating a very different response than the old belief. *Anything* creating tension, anxiety, or anger defeats you in your ability to operate within the zone of performance where you are most powerful.

ASK YOURSELF

1. What is your current state of tension? Are you as relaxed as you should be? If not, can you identify any performance indications related to your tension?

2. How are people around you? Do they become tense in your presence? Do you know?

3. Can you identify any important initiatives you are working on that you are less than relaxed about?

4. Can you identify the beliefs behind your tension? For example, do you believe this initiative is crucial to the success of the entire operation, is critical to your career, is highly visible, etc.....?

5. What percentage of your time do you operate at peak performance? (Note: there is a difference between constantly operating on the edge and in high tension, and operating at peak performance.)

In the table on the next page are examples of both the mundane and the complex problems which plague us. The examples will help you internalize what can be done with the beliefs to reframe your response. What you place in the last box must create a release of tension inside of you when you bring that thought into your mind. If the new belief you wrote in the last box does not create a release of tension, the new belief will not change the instinctive reaction you have to the event.

EVENT OR TRIGGER	BELIEF	NEW BELIEF (Examples)
Phone Interruptions	They are a distraction. What I am doing is more important. This call is a waste of my time.	I need a distraction and I didn't know it. The Universe shows me what's important. I need to pay attention. When I get back to what I was doing I will have new insights.
Criticism	It was unjust criticism. I'm not good enough. I'll never overcome this.	This will help me adjust my behavior in the future. God doesn't make junk. This is the feedback no one else had the guts to tell me.
Traffic Jams	I'll be late. I'm wasting time.	I'll get there at exactly moment I'm supposed to. I'm supposed to spend this time relaxing (one of my fundamentals of leadership).
Paperwork	Paperwork is boring. Paperwork is a waste of time.	I'll use the paperwork as an opportunity to review my week. This gives other ideas time to gel in my mind.

THINGS TO REMEMBER:

1. Check your breathing; take the time to adjust it!

2. Check and relax your muscles. Find a quiet place and practice your visualization.

3. Check your perspective:
   a. Are you deciding from fear?
   b. Are you making the decision in order to look good?
   c. Are you being controlled in some way by your beliefs?

CHAPTER III

RHYTHM

Rhythm is the next fundamental quality a person may focus on in a crisis. A person's rhythm is a function of his or her timing. When things become difficult, we often lose rhythm. Perhaps you have worked for people who seem to deliberate every issue until the moment for action is long past. Or perhaps your nemesis is the opposite type of boss or spouse or friend who seems to rush towards every challenge creating panic for those who must clean up the mess after the dust settles. In either situation, others suffer as the person struggles to assert his or her rhythm.

THE STORY

John walked into the board meeting in the best mood he had been in for months. As he walked through the lobby to the conference room, he nodded a greeting to the members of his staff who sat ready to answer questions or give presentations should the need arise. He was particularly aware of the amount of tension in the room. He had been unaware of the force of the tension until now. He seemed to have acquired an antenna for feeling stress in others since he recognized how destructive the stress had been to him.

Most of the board members were already present. He walked around the room shaking hands and greeting the men and women he had worked with and yet, in another sense, not worked with over the last three years. He spent a moment acknowledging the breadth and depth of the talent and experience represented in the room. As the last member, an elderly gentleman who, before his retirement, had run one of the world's largest chemical companies, entered the room, the group began the formal process of running the meeting.

After the formalities of reading minutes and covering the agenda were complete, the board sat expectantly waiting for the standard series of presentations to begin. John cleared his throat and said, "I'd really like to step outside of the normal expectations for this type of meeting today. As we all know, this company is in crisis, and we may need to do some extraordinary things to survive. I'd like to suggest a unique format for this meeting, as opposed to our traditional format."

Board member looked at board member. No one quite knew how to respond to what their CEO was saying. This clearly was not something they were expecting.

Sally, a woman in her late forties, was the first to react. "What do you have in mind, John?"

"It seems to me our whole way of doing business is making the problems worse. We are about to bring our top executives in here and demand answers to our problems when they do not know the answers. They've spent days creating presentations. We're good at inventing busy work that won't solve the problems. In fact, I look at my own decision-making style, and I've been working myself into a frenzy trying to come up with solutions I think will please you as well as solve the problems.

"Unfortunately, the solutions solving the problems aren't usually the ones I think will please you. The result is I lose my focus and begin making a lot of decisions prematurely, or find myself hesitating abnormally long on what might be helpful now."

Jim, a CFO at a Fortune 100 company, asked rather abruptly, "What are you saying? There are legal implications for the format here you know!"

"I know. I think our most important fiduciary responsibility is to make this company successful. I'm suggesting a problem-solving meeting utilizing all of the talent in this room to come up with the direction. In fact, I'm suggesting a whole new way of looking at decision-making. I'd really like to create an environment where solutions come from all of us."

Larry, the CEO of a consumer products company, had been frowning since John had challenged the format. "Just a minute. Are you admitting you don't have any answers? Perhaps you need to think about stepping aside and letting someone who does have answers take over."

John knew Larry's company was starting down the same path Sorot Corporation had traveled. John remained unruffled. He closed his eyes and gave thanks for his walk in the park before the meeting.

"You might think my stepping aside is a solution," he offered. "But I would disagree with you. No one knows this business better than I do. I have a proven track record. Perhaps I'm in over my head. Or maybe the real answers lie in how we arrive at the decisions. We've been trying to do what worked in the past. We have been unsuccessful. Maybe the events we're experiencing now are just what we need to shake us out of our complacency."

Joe, the chemical executive, suddenly sat up in his chair and agreed with John. "You know what John is saying not only shows extraordinary courage, but this approach shows wisdom as well. Month after month, we sit here listening to garbage, knowing what we're hearing is garbage, and the best we can do is come back and demand next quarter the numbers are better. If we're so smart, why are we sitting here listening? I would like to roll my sleeves up and go after this stuff. I'm sick to death of these boring, ineffective meetings. Let's grab those guys out in the other room and let's stay here until we get some answers! We can have the board meeting later, after we've made some progress."

"I just don't know," said Jim nervously. "We've never done this before. How do we know what the repercussions might be?"

Joe was disgusted. "Well, we're pretty clear about the consequences if we don't salvage this company. I guess I'd rather take some hits for not sticking to process than for losing our shareholders' investments."

After more quarreling, the more confident and domineering personalities were able to convince the others they could fulfill their responsibilities to the gathering of information and change the expectations of their role.

The executives in the outer room were invited in. They entered together with puzzled expressions overlying their tension. As John explained what they were about to do, the reactions were mixed. Several people began to grin. Jerry and Ned looked annoyed. Bob Skipper looked worried. Others had varying degrees of reaction from amused to concerned.

The board had appointed Joe to facilitate the meeting. As he stood at the easel, he was clearly enjoying himself.

"OK, let's get started. Perhaps we should make a list of our problems and then decide what we should look at first."

This part was easy. There was no shortage of problems. The list grew as the group talked. Many of the problems had existed for a long time.

John interrupted. "I'd like to suggest, before we begin to solve problems, we adopt a process for determining how we will approach them. I think we need a framework to determine whether our solutions are consistent and whether we are, in fact, following a predetermined path."

"What constitutes a framework?" asked Sally. "Are you thinking of a vision statement?"

"Yes, something like that. I'd like to go a little farther than a vision statement," replied John. "We spent months on a vision statement last year, but the work we did hasn't seemed to help much. I'm thinking more of defining how we will know whether we're on the right track."

Debbie spoke up. "You know, I think I understand what you mean. Especially in my work, I find when you look at the numbers long enough, they begin to lose their meaning. They become isolated facts rather than a complete system. How do I know, for example, whether cutting a specific cost fits with the rest of the business's needs? I can look at the bottom line and see a difference, but the organization seems to flounder. There is a lack of clarity about direction, and certainly a lack of clarity about how everything fits together.

"Exactly", said John. "If we make decisions without understanding what we are trying to create in terms of a feeling, we are very likely to create more chaos. I want to know just what kind of feeling we're trying to create with our customers, our employees, and all of our suppliers and distributors. I might find different ways to increase revenues."

"Okay," said Joe, taking control, "let's describe how we all want this thing to feel if we are, in fact, successful."

Jerry and Ned rolled their eyes and a few of the others shifted uncomfortably in their chairs. Sally and Debbie immediately began to give their ideas to Joe.

◆ ◆ ◆ ◆ ◆ ◆

THE FUNDAMENTAL

Rhythm

Rhythm is a form of measured movement. When an entity has rhythm, it has a grace and harmony. Decision-making has a definite rhythm. If you could step back and view *you* from a distance, would you see a pattern indicative of a wonderful sense of timing and pace? Or would you see irregular fits of stopping and starting?

You may observe times when your rhythm is good and other times when it is not. Others observe the same things, perhaps more sensitively than you do yourself. Your sense of timing will have a great deal to do with your ability to inspire trust.

The Connection Between Risk and Rhythm

Unfortunately, circumstances will often conspire to force us into decisions we are not ready to make. To predict the impact of choices is difficult, if not impossible. To do so when you are feeling the pressure of troublesome times is even more demanding.

The most important factor in determining the pacing of the decisions is your perception of the risks involved. If you perceive a risk in making a certain type of decision, you are likely to hesitate, sometimes too long. If you are afraid others are incapable of making decisions or if you are afraid of waiting to make a decision until all of the facts are available, this, too, is an example of acting on a *perceived* risk. In situations where you act too quickly or wait too long, the inclination of the observer is to believe you are not in control.

A fear or risk affecting your pace or rhythm of decision-making is often hidden within beliefs not even acknowledged. For example, John admitted to the board he was being forced into making decisions too soon because he was worried they might think he was incapable of making a decision. His perception was not totally inaccurate. There was an undeniable risk in standing up in front of the board and admitting he did not have the answers.

Those who rush at decisions or those who deliberate excessively usually do not realize the cause is an unidentified fear. *Everyone* has timing problems occasionally. When the timing issue becomes a pattern, a fear is usually operating subliminally. The ability to *manage* the fear is often the differentiation between powerful people and ineffective people.

SYMPTOMS

Good self-assessment of personal rhythm is very difficult. In the most extreme cases of rhythm problems, the timing difficulty is usually accompanied by a sense of being uncentered or off-balance. You know something is wrong because you can not think clearly and you feel as though you are moving sluggishly or being rushed.

The world appears horribly chaotic at such times. The person has a feeling of being out of control and near the edge. Often, people describe the feeling as being fragmented and pulled in too many directions. The feeling of being "pulled apart at the seams" is an indication rhythm is being drastically affected. This feeling reveals a lack of stability permeating the leader's capacity to make good decisions.

Another symptom of rhythm imbalance is in the quality of the decision. If a decision is reached when the rhythm is out of sync, the results of the decision often do not work out well. A decision reached prematurely will frequently result in rework. A decision reached too slowly will be offered too late to create the desired objective. The world has already moved on.

Two of the most common forms of imbalance in rhythm are impatience and lethargy. Each is important enough to merit attention.

A. Impatience

Impatience is usually accompanied by abruptness and anxiety. The individual is afraid something will be taken away if he or she does not move quickly. There is a need to act immediately, often ignoring the requirement to gather data and support.

Impatient people are the ones who can not wait until morning to start something they think of in the night. They often abuse others by calling them at strange hours. Given a position of power, they will habitually insist others respond immediately to their needs. They usually will not inquire into the convenience for the other person. They assume the other person is duty-bound to respond to their sense of urgency.

Impatient people frequently have little balance in their own lives and often presume others are the same. They start or finish projects on evenings or weekends with little regard for the lifestyles or needs of others who must respond because *they* perceive they have no choice. The world must revolve around their sense of urgency. If the world does not revolve around impatient people, or if they can not reach a person when they want to, the impatient person will often respond with anger. Usually, because the anger is so visible and intense, others will cancel everything to react.

The people responding to the anger will throw their lives out of balance to meet the needs of the impatient person. Entire schedules or project plans will be contorted to avoid the anger. Efficiency is destroyed, making the impatient decision-maker even more frantic. Rarely does this person realize he or she is a primary cause for the lack of completion which becomes an ongoing theme in the person's life.

The person who responds to this urgency in others is often reacting with his or her own version of impatience. This person, too, is afraid; afraid of disappointing or being viewed as uncooperative. The alternative might be for this victim of the impatient person to simply say, "I'm busy right now, but I'll be with you as soon as I can." The measured response would be to finish what is at hand and then respond.

There are many symptoms to help a person identify if he or she is one of those who must learn to temper impatience. The first symptom is a trail of unfinished brainstorms. The person's subconscious is aware of the trail of unfinished business even if he or she appears to be oblivious. The cycle of unfinished business escalates because as the person feels the need to create a win, the sense of urgency becomes even greater.

Impatience manifesting in rudeness or shortness is symptomatic of a rhythm problem. Why? There is a clock in the mind of the impatient person constantly measuring the passage of time. Normally, this person would not want to be thought of as rude or short, but the "situation" demands he or she act with urgency. A well-paced person has no need to be rude or short to prove his or her point. He or she has time to solve the problem differently.

The rudeness or shortness is a symptom of a deeper problem. Others are cut off, seemingly because their ideas have no merit. More realistically, the leader has a fear that he or she will somehow lose ground with his or her own idea by listening to the ideas of others.

In John's case, for example, he was feeling forced into making decisions he was not ready to make. He was making premature decisions because of his fear of not looking good to the board. Members of the board were rude and insulting to John rather than waiting to see where his thoughts were leading. In the board members' case, the lack of patience was due to their fear of being led down the wrong path or wasting time.

B. Lethargy

The antithesis of impatience is lethargy. Lethargic people are those individuals who appear as though anyone can "roll over" them like a tank because they are too ineffective to stand up for themselves. These are the leaders who anger us because they do not step into the fight soon enough and often leave others "holding the bag."

Lethargic people are not just slow with decisions. Lethargic people are slow to act in general. As a result, they appear to be lacking in substance. They appear to have no courage or moral fiber. Perhaps they suggest an idea and then retreat when the idea is ill-received. As a leader, this person might allow his or her subordinates to take beatings publicly for things he or she originally suggested.

Lethargy might also appear as a lack of communication skills. This person has trouble making a point. He or she is frequently not taken seriously. In short, this person appears to lack passion.

Other symptoms of lethargy are a lack of follow-through or a seeming lack of a sense of direction. These symptoms of people whose rhythm is functioning on the lethargic side are usually based on fear. Often the fear is hidden. Frequently the fear is of appearing too pushy or too obnoxious. These are typically people who have learned to hate the affect of the impatient types and use this dislike to justify inaction.

Stagnation is a symptom of lethargy. Decisions are remade or not made in countless meetings. One executive described this stagnation as feeling like he was reliving the movie *Groundhog Day*. In the movie, a man is forced to relive the same day hundreds of times until he gets the day right. Perhaps we are all forced to live our own version of *Groundhog Day* until we understand that the magic to making decisions in a timely way lies within our sense of self.

LESSONS LEARNED BY POWERFUL PEOPLE

Any person can have problems with deciding too quickly or too slowly. The ability to make timely decisions often depends on the moment and what fear is affecting the person's choices. Rhythm problems are symptoms of the person's lack of confidence with the specific situation. If rushing or excessive deliberation becomes a pattern, the problem must be addressed as a root problem. If the symptom of impatience or lethargy appears only sporadically, as opposed to an overall pattern of behavior, identify the cause within the specific situation generating the impatience or the lethargy. "What about this particular issue is causing me to be off balance?"

If you were walking across an unstable bridge with no handrails high above a mountain stream, you might have moments of anxiety causing you to rush or to move incredibly slowly. If the bridge were, in fact, unstable enough to be dangerous, the rushing or stalling could be deadly. For the traveler on such a bridge, the addition of handrails would help establish a safer rhythm. For a person in an organization or situation racked by uncertainty, a similar frame is needed. The frame will not solve the problem of the uncertainty or instability, but a structure will give the person a stronger sense of direction within which to make the decisions.

Creating a Frame

Mature people often create a picture of the desired outcome in their minds as they examine an issue. They habitually create a vision for every decision, from the mundane to the complex.

Creating an image of the desired outcome is a discipline. The leader must slow down and ask the question, "How would this look and feel if the situation were perfect?" The inclusion of how the desired result *feels* is key to arriving at a complete answer.

Once a person has taken the time to think through how the outcome would look and feel, the paths to the solutions become much clearer. If, for example, the problem is a recurring service problem, a picture of the perfect outcome would include happy employees, responsive suppliers, satisfied *and* fair customers and a quality product.

The *completeness* of the picture, including the happy employees, might encourage the leader to include fresh options in the solution. Without the complete vision, for example, a person might institute a dozen new forms of control making the employees' ability to serve the customer much harder. This type of over-controlling happens continuously in organizations.

The picture provides a direction inclusive of the entire system because a picture puts the problem-solving in a *context*. Without the visual, the person may make decisions to solve the immediate crisis creating more crises as a result. The person appears to be out of rhythm, but, in reality, he or she was simply thinking too narrowly about the outcome.

For many powerful people, the use of visualization to solve problems is a spontaneous, subliminal process. When questioned about why they arrive at the solutions, these people usually describe a picture which includes *a sense of the whole*. Powerful people are operating from a context that includes *all* of the variables, and hence they seem to have a certain "luck" in their results. Is it luck or is this ability to identify successful paths perhaps a greater feel for where and how things fit together.

Using visualization to create a sense of context is very helpful in developing better instincts for decision-making. Visualization is similar in effect to placing handrails on the unstable bridge.

ASK YOURSELF

The following questions will help you think about whether you have a rhythm issue. Note: others are part of the equation to good decision-making when you are acting as a leader. It is not enough to simply make good decisions.

1. Do others argue with you when you decide on a course of action? Do they get frustrated trying to make you understand why it won't work?

2. Have you been accused of being arrogant, as if you think your decisions are better than the decisions of others?

3. Do others comment on your not including others in your thinking processes for decision-making? Do they feel as if you "get there" all by yourself and then expect them to just go along?

4. Do you ask or expect others to work during non-business hours often?

5. Are you often short with others? Do you make excuses for your shortness? Are you short with your family members but not others? Are you feeling like being short, but force yourself to be polite? (Note: they will intuitively feel your impatience even if you work hard to disguise it)

6. Before you implement a decision, do you visualize the result you expect? Do you include in your visualization the way others will feel and respond when the decisions is implemented perfectly?

The meeting continued in the board room. Jackie had dinner brought in and the group continued to develop their image of a healthy, successful company. There were some surprises along the way making them realize some of the reasons for their struggle.

The picture which evolved as they described what they wanted included customers who liked working with them. In their vision customers and suppliers alike sought their advice and worked in cooperation with them to help them determine what to provide in the way of service. Employees were enthusiastic and willing to offer help. No one worked in a silo. Everyone looked for ways to share resources to create the best overall outcome.

"You know," said Joe, as he stepped back and looked at the list, "I'm not sure we still know what to do to solve all of the problems. But I am sure of one thing. The things we have been doing have actually worked against this picture of the problem 'solved.' We've squeezed employees again and again without asking their advice. We've created a potential turf war with our executives, as we've demanded that each of them clean up their area without even talking about how their decisions will affect the whole. And we've made all of our customers mad, because in trying to cut costs, we've cut out important things. We ask them what they want, but do we know how to listen?"

"What do you mean?" asked Debbie. "We have council meetings all the time with our key customers."

"Sure we do. But why do things keep getting worse? Maybe they don't know how to tell us what they really want and we're not smart enough to listen. Maybe their objections aren't really about price. We keep cutting price and they keep getting madder. I think we need to think about whether we are taking the time to determine what they really mean. Every time we cut price, we need to take something out of our costs that makes them mad. Perhaps we need to figure out how to give them more of what they want so price is less of the issue."

Jerry spoke for the first time since he had sat down. "Perhaps you forget we're in a highly competitive environment," he said sarcastically. "These smiling faces are all very nice, but you still have to deal with reality."

"I simply know we will not have a successful company until the picture we have created becomes real," responded Joe with no sense of having been attacked. "I think we need to direct our efforts and I think we'd better start trying to figure out how, now."

"We have to survive now!" Ned said in a high-pitched voice. For some reason, the discussion was creating a feeling of panic in Ned. All this talk about pictures felt like time lost in surviving.

"You know, Ned," responded John, "we've been making our decisions by trying to survive for quite a while. We seem to continually lose ground. I'm actually relieved to see another frame for making our decisions. Perhaps we need to focus on thriving as well as surviving. I, for one, am eager to get on with repairing some bridges we may have burned in our panic. Since everything else we seem to do is backfiring, I think changing our approach at least offers us a place to start."

"It makes me realize why our efficiency efforts have been so disastrous," said Joe. "We never even asked our employees how we could be more efficient. We brought in high-priced consultants to tell us what every employee knows. And we made the people who are our front line to the customer mad. Really mad. I guess I would have been mad, too. Now we have union problems to deal with in our next negotiations. What will our oversights cost us then?"

"Well, I certainly see some places to start now," said

John. "I vote we adjourn and give me and my team a few days to work through some things in terms of our current projects and initiatives to see if we can't fit our solutions into this picture better."

Jerry had the last word as everyone organized themselves to leave. "Well, I will be very interested to see what the numbers are next quarter, when we're spending all this time on making people feel good."

◆ ◆ ◆ ◆ ◆ ◆

MORE LESSONS LEARNED

Strong people develop their rhythm over time. Rhythm can be adjusted by adjusting the way you think. Knowing where to start is the secret.

A. Using Reality

Creating an image of a perfect outcome provides a greater sense of stability for the person, but imaging does *not* determine the *path* to the outcome. The decisions must still be made. How should a person determine the appropriate course and speed of action? *Within* the frame of the vision the individual can *begin* to develop a rhythm for powerful decisions. The resolution of rhythm problems is determined by the actions which follow the visioning step.

The dilemma in making the choices to arriving at the vision is the predicament Jerry and Ned point out. Jerry and Ned represent reality. They represent the fear and nay-saying in the organization discouraging a leader from operating from a vision.

Go *with* the flow rather than fight the elements representing reality. Jerry and Ned are part of the decision process. When constrained by any reality, the rule is to find a way to make the reality work *in favor of* whatever outcome you are trying to achieve.

Finding a way to make the concerns felt by Jerry and Ned part of the solution is key to John's success in decision-making. To ignore the concerns or work against them is fatal. The solution *must* contain elements to help Sorot survive *and* thrive. John needs to create an outcome which includes Jerry and Ned. This does not mean he waits for them to agree with him. He must acknowledge and factor in their concerns.

Timing is another critical factor in utilizing reality to make decisions. If today's decisions are irrelevant tomorrow, you must factor that understanding into all solutions. What advantages does so little certainty in the future give? If life is changing rapidly, you may actually have more influence on the direction of the change than when life is changing slowly. The rapid pace of change actually offers opportunity to make a significant difference.

For example, a fast growing company often will struggle with naive and inexperienced work-force issues. If the leader asks, "How can I make this work for me instead of against me?", a variety of insights might emerge. Perhaps being naive makes the individuals better listeners. They have not heard all the reactions. They are fresh and therefore, possibly, more open. The inexperience might make them more innovative at a time when innovation is badly needed. Many advantages might be leveraged if the leadership looks at inexperience as a strength rather than a deficit.

The decisions the leader makes will be different if he or she values naive as a strength. The formula is to take every resource and utilize the resource in the most powerful way to achieve the desired outcome.

Use reality. Do not waste precious time bemoaning what is. Regret is a useless waste of energy.

B. Anticipate the Patterns

If you pay attention to the incremental changes in the environment, you are more able to control the direction of the flow. By being prepared to react quickly at both an intellectual and physical level, you can make choices proactively you might otherwise feel have been thrust upon you. Watching the movement of others and predicting their direction, knowing the desired outcome and using *all* of the information to develop a strategy, puts you in control of the rhythm and tone of the outcomes.

To achieve real rhythm, you must train yourself to do two things. You must predict the future and you must learn to act deliberately to control your destiny. The ability to predict direction is what makes a decision timely as opposed to rushed. If the leader is skilled at anticipating the movement of others, he or she is never creating decisions which throw people off balance. The leader is in perfect sync with events and the decisions appear simply as the natural order of things.

The first step to predicting accurately is to understand how people think. We often make mistakes in business based on our assumptions about what the customer wants. For example, do you know what your customers' biggest concerns are? Most organizations know what the customer's buying patterns have been. Do you know the kinds of things shaping their future? Unless you have identified their concerns, you do not know the very significant influences steering them off the course you predicted from their past choices.

If you know what your customers' concerns are, do you know what your company's concerns *should* be? Are you anticipating those concerns as you envision your future choices. In other words, are you making decisions based on what is happening now versus what happened two or three years ago?

1. Are you fighting with reality rather than using it to your advantage? Mentally, make a list of the things most frustrating to you. Try to create ways of looking at each of the things on your list that turn the item into an advantage.

2. Are you fighting egos? How can you make the egos work for you instead of against you? What will you need to let go of in order to do so?

3. List all of the people who are critical to your success. What do you know about what is important to them?

3. Are there patterns affecting your work right now that could have been anticipated? Are there patterns emerging as you read this that will affect your work in the future? Are you adjusting for them or waiting?

MORE LESSONS LEARNED

C. Allowing the Flight

When you are not sure of the direction, admit it, stand still, and allow events to unfold. They will! Unfortunately, too often people try to force the future in the direction they want and pay no attention to the symptoms telling them they are on the wrong path.

If what you are doing is not working, the wise person is quiet until the correct path emerges. When decisions and initiatives do not work out the way people wish, things often take on a frantic tone. People push for answers others do not have. The pressure is intense for immediate action.

If you want to be effective and to find answers, do not ask for any! Think about what is happening and what the chain of events occurring now means. Identify what messages are trying to emerge from the chaos. Play with different ways to create your future. Do not react before it is clear. The wrong move could be devastating.

ASK YOURSELF

1. Are you attempting to force answers when you are not *absolutely certain* that your path is the correct path? (You must be very honest with yourself as you answer this question. Often people assume they are supposed to have answers and attempt to make the rest of the world believe they do even when they do not.)

2. Have you made decisions that became poor decisions because of unfolding events you could not have predicted? If so, were you forcing or hurrying the decision when you were not completely certain it was the right decision?

3. Are you inclined to make any decision rather than no decision when you are not sure? Do you get impatient with others who won't make a decision? Could you be wrong?

THE STORY

Jerry, Ned, Debbie, Jackie, Bob, and John were sitting in John's office. They were talking about what to do next. Ned and Jerry felt the board meeting had been a waste of time and had not held back in sharing their beliefs.

"Well, we still need to determine some next steps," said John. "I actually feel better than I have in a while. I at least think I know where to start."

"And where is that?" asked Bob. "I'm not any clearer than I was before."

"We need to find out what's on our customers' minds. Not with focus groups or with meetings where we tell them what we are going to do next and ask their opinion. We need to find out what they want!"

"I could ask a few of them to come here to talk to us," said Bob, grateful to at last have a direction that did not put him on the defensive. "Some of our customers are still loyal even though they're telling us they're not happy."

"Get a meeting set up," said John. "I also want to see a list of our cost cutting initiatives," he told Debbie. "I want to see how they all fit into our image of a healthy, vital company. I need to see exactly where we are losing money and where we are gaining. I want to see if there are any patterns I haven't noticed before because I wasn't looking for them."

"What do you mean?" asked Debbie.

"I'm looking for trends in terms of what customers want. We always try to recapture what we're losing rather than try to figure out what the information might be telling us about the future."

John turned to Ned next. "Ned, I want to see a list of all the legal attacks we've had in the last 12 months. I'm looking for things to do with employee lawsuits as well as customer or supplier charges."

"Why?" asked Ned, his curiosity piqued in spite of himself. He could not resist the personal power John was exhibiting.

"Because we're going to look at the obvious things our employees, customers, and suppliers are telling us about what we're doing wrong. Next we'll go after the more subtle

stuff. I can not get the picture of cooperation out of my mind from our exercise with the board, and I know we're not there."

"I suppose you have an assignment for me, too?" asked Jerry.

"You and I need to look at some of the efficiency efforts we're making and determine how we can mold them to create cooperation with the employees. We may need to go out and talk to some of the local union members as well. There is so much we have not listened to. We need to start. We've missed a lot, but if we're lucky, and we move fast, we may not be too late. We've been so anxious just to be doing something, I fear we've been acting without the right information."

MORE LESSONS LEARNED

D. Leverage the Mistakes

Sometimes your decisions will be wrong. No one is perfect and if we expend enormous energy trying to avoid mistakes, we are likely to create fearful, disorganized, risk-averters. How, then, do you create an environment that embraces change rather than fears mistakes?

Continual honesty with yourself and your motives is critical. Watch the patterns of your decisions. Are you holding back because of fear? When a decision goes wrong, do you react with dismay or anger?

The objective is to achieve a sense of rhythm in the decisions you make each day. Acknowledging and working with reality, anticipating the patterns, and allowing things to unfold until they are clearer are all techniques for managing the *fear* of mistakes. The next challenge is to manage the *consequences* of a bad decision. The ability to handle the outcomes of a poor choice with grace and fearlessness are determining factors in preparing to make the *next* decision.

Mistakes happen. The most productive thing to do is to put energy into imagining what happened was inevitable and asking where the choice was meant to guide you. In other words, what positive outcome will happen *only* because you or others made the choice? Amazing creativity comes from such an attitude.

If the mistake is a product that does not sell, or a marketing plan that does not work, or a public relations faux pas, or a career or life choice that does not work out, how can you leverage the mistake in your favor? To ask what larger mistake might be looming (and avoidable because of what you have learned), is far more beneficial than belaboring the poor judgment that created the problem. Identify a path you or your company is on that would not have happened any other way.

"What *direction* has this event pointed to?" is also a constructive question. To develop a discipline for thinking about errors as a part of the path will create a much different climate in the organization. Learning from mistakes is important. Learning from the outcome of bad choices is empowering rather than destructive.

Many "mistakes" happen in a pattern. Determine how the mistake fits into the optimal direction of the organization. You will be more comfortable confronting your blunders. You will be more likely to pay attention to the *symptoms* of wrong choices.

When, and if, you allow yourself and others the room to believe the mistakes are all part of leading you somewhere, the process of learning and growing becomes fun again. Others will follow your example.

Learn to operate from the assumption you are *not* here to be perfect. You are here to *react* perfectly. Reacting perfectly means using each incremental step to help you understand what the next step should be. Broken down into the smaller steps, miscalculations become bite-size. They cease to create the negative result of individuals, including yourself, clinging to being right because of the consequences of being wrong.

ASK YOURSELF

1. If you examine what you believe to be your largest failure, do you blame yourself for not recognizing some important element necessary for success?

2. What would you do differently today?

3. Can you imagine a project or initiative you may be responsible for in the future or currently where the consequences are more important than the one on which you failed? How will you use what you have learned?

4 Can you see any advantage to having learned on the previous issue rather than now? Would you still go back and have the other situation turn out differently if it meant you would not have your current understandings?

THINGS TO REMEMBER

1. **If you find your rhythm is off, identify the perceived threat or risk affecting your decisions.**

2. **If you find a lack of completion in your life, either in a form of too many unfinished projects or in an ambivalence to start projects, the ambivalence or**

the lack of completion are symptoms of a rhythm issue.

3. To improve your rhythm, visualize your desired out come *before* you take action. Be sure all action fits within the vision.

4. Stay alert to the patterns in people's thinking which will tell you what priorities are important!

5. Allow things to unfold if you are not clear.

6. Use mistakes to your advantage.

CHAPTER IV

FREEDOM

Freedom, in the context of developing individual and leadership capacity, is represented by an ability to move unfettered; unencumbered by fear. Freedom is the ability to judge one's self and one's actions against a set of values, as compared to the thoughts or opinions of others. This is the next evolution beyond relaxation and rhythm of your understanding of your capacity for risk. As the individual evolves in his or her capacity to move freely, the techniques for decision-making learned in the development of rhythm become ingrained to the point of being instinctive. You automatically relax yourself in tense situations. You instinctively create an opportunity in your head out of every crisis. As a result of your ability to take action irrespective of the opinions of others, you become known as a maverick.

THE STORY

Bob slipped into John's office unannounced. John was reading some of the reports Jerry had provided regarding the efficiency studies. As John looked up, Bob sat down heavily, running his hands nervously through his hair.

"What's up?" asked John, taking off his glasses and looking directly at him.

"I talked to most of our major customers. They were blunt. They say we have not kept up, we missed the mark with our product designs, and we're really behind in the quality issues. Each one of them could tell me about major

shipments of parts sent back because our parts failed in the tests they run on their products. I was pretty discouraged. And the things they talked about were all things I can't control. I wish some of the other guys would listen to these customers. What's Jerry doing to control the quality, anyway? We hear the same garbage every week at our meetings and nothing seems to improve."

"Well, I agree we have a problem with quality. I'm not sure the problem is all Jerry's problem. We all seem to want to blame someone. Bob, are you willing to pull all these customers together to talk to our entire team?"

"I don't know. That seems pretty risky to me. If we put them all in the same room and let them vent, we're likely to see them all walk out the door at the same time."

"Yes, we certainly are," said John. "They may walk anyway. There may be a pattern to the quality problems we're just not seeing. We take in all the data but we never seem to get at the root of the problem. Our customers have the answers and we're not doing anything about retrieving the information. I feel as if we may need to take a risk."

"Jerry will never agree to do a meeting with the customers. A meeting with customers would leave him so exposed."

"Jerry may be getting more comfortable with the risk involved. We've already gone through some of the problems with the employees over the last week. We went out and talked to them in groups and really got an earful. At first, Jerry was very tense and defensive, but after a while he started to listen. The employees were really only talking about being treated with respect. They wanted to be valued for what they were doing and to feel the company had some sort of loyalty to them. We had some real down to earth discussions about what that would look like and feel like."

"Did they have anything to say about the quality or the back order problems we're experiencing?" asked Bob.

"Actually, they said they had a lot of helpful information, but they wanted to have more trust in us before they participated in solving the problems. They wanted to know we wouldn't use the information to eliminate jobs or increase our profits without sharing the rewards."

"That might be a problem. Isn't our role always to increase the margins for our stockholders? If we see ways to make more money, we'd be wrong not to."

"I'm not sure we haven't lost sight of our overall objective. Increasing margins has ruled us for a long time. Look where we are. Even if the margins were less, but the company was growing and stable, aren't we doing more for the stockholders than if we make all our employees mad by creating decisions that make us look good in the short-term?"

"I don't know," said Bob. "Our job security depends on the way we look now, not later."

"I need to step up to that," said John thoughtfully. AI need to start thinking about what the right thing to do is, rather than how I look in the eyes of the stockholders. They're not as close to this. All they have are the numbers. But I have the responsibility of all the employees and the health of the company. I don't think I've been a very good steward over the last two years. I was too caught up in looking good. I'm rethinking all our employee and supplier policies from the viewpoint of how I keep these relationships healthy. I'm going to do what I think is right and deal with the consequences. I hope to get the whole team to do the same, but the first move has to begin with me."

"Good luck," said Bob wearily. "I, for one, need to go put a meeting together."

John smiled as Bob left the room.

THE FUNDAMENTAL

Freedom

Freedom is elusive. Most of us like to think we are independent of others. And yet, you must look closely at your patterns of thinking and behaving. For example, when you are confronted with a crisis, where does your mind first travel? Do you think of the implications of the crisis on your career? Do you think of the reactions of others? Imagine the mental freedom of not needing to think of anything but the solution to the problem.

The Connection Between Risk-Taking and Freedom

Freedom: "the ease or facility of movement or action." For a person to operate with a sense of freedom, he or she must first learn to control reactions to perceived threat. A person must control what is happening internally.

We interpret the world through our beliefs. We have learned to fear the results of certain outcomes. Those fears are integrated into our beliefs about how the world works. Our ability to understand those fears and manage the beliefs surrounding them is a fundamental quality of mastery.

In many respects we are trained in opposition to the qualities of mastery. We fear uncertainty. We fear crisis. We are trained to attempt to remain totally in control of outcomes. No surprises. Everything must be predictable. We avoid situations we can not anticipate. We fear failure. We are not built to be strong, confident creatures in the face of adversity. To be strong and confident are basics we must relearn.

Often, we are trained to consider the expectations of others before we determine a course of action. The more we value the opinions of others, the less freedom we have. If we are honest with ourselves, the concept of making decisions without regarding the opinions of others is very threatening.

The difference lies in the balance and the degree. To what degree are we letting the opinions of others, or our fear of their opinions, deter us from doing what is right?

Bob was fearful of putting a room full of customers together. The customers' reactions were unpredictable. John, having grown through so many of the issues around rhythm and relaxation, was taking the next step in his own evolution. John was becoming more and more comfortable with exposing himself to negative feedback in his need to get answers. Finding the answers had become more important than avoiding criticism. Unfortunately, many members of the staff did not feel the same.

John, too, had been concerned with the reaction of the board members and the customers in the past. Perhaps he had even been afraid of the reactions of his own staff to his decisions. He had become ineffective. The most difficult risk for many individuals to manage is losing face or position.

John points out the obvious when he suggests he must learn to do the right thing even if the right thing is not what others want him to do. More subtly, he asks his team to stand in front of others and invite open feedback. Why did this seem so daunting to Bob?

Freedom is achieved by taking risk. Risk-takers are those who analyze a situation, make a determination of what will bring them closer to a desired outcome and move forward in spite of the potential for things to go wrong. Successful risk-takers not only confront the risk, but they manage the risk in order to diminish the potential damage. Leaders do not hesitate at critical moments. They move toward their future rather than waiting for the future to happen to them.

Whatever the dragon, risk-takers acknowledge the problem and meet the problem head on. They do not pretend the dragon does not exist, nor do they become overwhelmed by the size of the beast. To be overwhelmed and immobilized by concern indicates a lack of freedom.

We know the results of risk-taking, even if we struggle to define what we mean by the term "risk-taking." There are clues to tell us when risk-taking exists in an organization. There are usually high states of energy, high states of optimism and high levels of personal confidence. Where these qualities are missing, risk-taking is also absent.

SYMPTOMS

A lack of freedom may have many manifestations. Freedom's absence may be indicated by a lack of flexibility or innovation. Are you willing to try new ideas?

Another symptom of a lack of freedom is a fear of challenging authority. Telling a higher level person he or she is wrong is simply not done in many organizations. Fear of honest communication can become a part of the culture. Cultures fearing honest communication often become passive-aggressive C back-stabbing and sabotage become the routine.

If you blame the culture for your problems, however, you must remember culture is determined by individual responses. If you personally choose not to challenge authority because of the culture, the choice is a symptom of a lack of development of your personal sense of freedom. The culture should be seen as a test

61

rather than a determining factor. Risk-taking is mostly attitude. Your personal view of risk-taking is a question of degree. Something you consider a great risk, another person may react to as though the same set of circumstances were inconsequential.

Another indication of a lack of freedom can be found in a person's schedule. Are you overwhelmed, constantly feeling you don't have enough time to do everything expected of you? The question is, why don't you say "No"? Often, an overwhelming schedule reflects a person's fear of disappointing others.

Question any sort of "victim" mentality C in yourself or others. Would a true risk-taker use budget as an excuse for not doing things, or would he or she find a way around financial constraints? The saddest reflection of a lack of freedom is exhibited by the person who has lost integrity. Are you doing things you believe to be ethically or morally wrong because what you are doing is expected of you? Do you feel your integrity has been victimized by the situation?

ASK YOURSELF

1. Are you a risk-taker? On a scale of one to ten, with ten being high, what level of risk taker are you?

2. Is there anything you believe you or your organization is doing that is wrong? Is it treating its labor force well? Does the organization treat people fairly? Have you ever felt that you were forced to treat an employee badly due to the organization's policies? Personally, have you treated others badly because of a belief about their worth? If so, think specifically about your response. What inhibitions, if any, did you have to speaking out for what was right? What were your concerns?

3. Are you happy in your work? Are you happy in your life? If not, what are you doing to change it? Is there anything holding you back from making significant change? What is it?

4. Are you a hero? If you were, what would you be doing that you are not doing right now?

5. Is there an element of the culture of your organization you dislike? Examine your own behaviors to see where you might be exhibiting the same behavior. If you were to drop the behavior and act counter-culturally, what would that feel like? Examine your perception of the risks.

LESSONS LEARNED BY POWERFUL PEOPLE

A. The Role of Judgment

Freedom is not just taking risk. Freedom is taking risks with *judgment*. Judgment is an ability to make a decision or form an opinion objectively, authoritatively and wisely, especially in matters affecting action. Good judgment also reflects discretion and good sense. Freedom does *not* occur when the leader is taking *indiscriminate* actions causing more problems than positive results.

Often, the really superb leader is a person who does not perceive what he or she is doing as risky. The powerful leader *knows* what is being attempted will work. He or she has weighed the negative consequences and dismissed them either because the consequences are tolerable or because the potentially negative repercussions of the decision will *probably* not be realized. The tolerance for what others perceive as risky is much greater because the highly effective person has factored the consequences of *not* taking the action into the equation and has decided the greater risk is not to act.

The powerful individual has developed a certainty over time due to a history of making sound decisions. How does a person develop certainty? How does the person override the voices stopping others from taking the risk? How is the strong individual able to combine sureness with a sense of judgment which improves the odds of being right more often than being wrong? What makes one person's guesses less inhibited and more accurate than another person's?

Judgment is not a gift. Judgment is developed over time, usually subconsciously. However, discretion and discrimination can be actively cultivated. The first step to cultivating judgment is to understand and manage fear.

The most significant improvement in a leader's skill in judgment is achieved by developing the intuitive skills. When the leader is alert to the challenge of managing personal fear, he or she can then focus on evolving the ability to analyze and predict outcomes more effectively through the use of intuition. Unfortunately, intuition is inaccessible when fear is present.

B. The Impact of Fear

Often, people are capable of better judgment than they exhibit. An individual may have a wonderful sense of what the right thing to do is in any given situation, and yet consistently exhibit behavior that appears to be void of judgment. Is the person really lacking in judgment or is he or she just too fearful to act on the right alternative?

Knowing what you and others fear will help you separate the

issue of judgment from non-action. When you are failing to respond in a manner you know is appropriate, ask yourself what your greatest concern is. Then ask yourself what you would do if the concern was removed as a threat.

This is a good exercise to test the "judgment" of others as well. Question individuals on how they might handle a situation if any perceived threat were removed. If you find their instincts are good, you may find your biggest task is to help them work through the fears.

Too often we rationalize our immobility by making excuses. We say the reason we can not react is because of our boss, the company, the economy, the budget, etc. If we really wanted to get "it" done, we would. Results, unfortunately, often mirror *intentions*.

What are the most common fears subtly getting in our way? The fear of calling negative attention to ourselves is the most common fear. Behind the fear is often hidden the fear of getting on some list making your job or promotability less secure. "Losing face" becomes equal in your subconscious mind to losing your job or your momentum in the act of climbing up the food chain.

First, you must decide if you want to be a slave to the fear of losing your career momentum. Losing face becomes less important when you decide you would rather live fully than live in constant fear of being viewed poorly. Clearly, the level of personal responsibility you have will affect your answers to questions of this nature. The size of your mortgage, your family commitments, etc. all impact your ability to live freely.

Second, if your action is frowned upon, what are the odds of *really* damaging your career? Examine this question relative to time. If you lose momentum, is the loss temporary or forever?

What does a temporary loss of momentum by taking action for the right reasons do to your long-term momentum? The questions you ask yourself first are related to what you are really afraid of. The second step is to question whether your fears are legitimate in the larger picture. Our organizations are filled with people who have recovered from their political mistakes to move on. Those who learn a pattern of risk-averse action, however, tend to plateau more permanently later in their careers.

Some fears are over-dramatizations of what could happen. The real costs of *not* acting may be much greater than your internal dramas. If you are afraid of looking bad and spoiling your options for the future, perhaps you should look at what those options will be if your personal situation or your company goes rapidly downhill due to poor decisions. This has become a reality for many people. We become protective of our careers and our life and our organizations stop moving forward as a result.

ASK YOURSELF

1. On a scale of one to ten with one being low and ten being high, how much do you value your current life-style?

2. How would you feel about telling your family you were going to pull back and live differently? (NOTE: The strength of your answers will usually be directly related to your willingness to take risks.)

3. How important is it others think well of you? This is a very significant question. The question is not "do they think well of your work?" The question is "do they think well of you as a person?"

    (If having others think well of you as a person means that you will do what makes others like you even if the action

you take is the wrong choice, you are inhibiting your freedom of action in order to create the right impressions.)

4. How much of your need to have others think well of you
   is career related, and how much is that you have a personal need to be liked?

THE STORY

Jerry was furious. He had been pacing in John's office
for ten minutes venting his feelings about the meeting Bob
was putting together.

"Why would he do anything so foolish? Can he possibly
realize the consequences of putting all those people in the
same room? We're likely to look like the biggest group of
idiots since time began!"

"What are you most afraid of?" asked John.

"I'm not afraid. If I were afraid, would I be talking to
you like this?" asked Jerry. "I'm mad. What he's doing
lacks common sense."

"Why?" persisted John. "What could possibly happen?"

"I can't believe you're asking that," said Jerry. "If they
get started, they're going to get really carried away and
you're going to hear about every little thing we've done
wrong in the last ten years. This meeting could turn into a
trounce Sorot party."

"Perhaps we need to hear every little thing we've done
wrong in the last ten years," said John. "I'm even thinking
about inviting some of the employees to the meeting."

"Are you crazy?" demanded Jerry. "I can't believe you!"

"Look," said John with amusement. "We are about to
go bankrupt. You may think a customer meeting is tough. I
think losing all of our jobs and the jobs of our employees
because we don't have the guts to hear the truth is tougher.
I'm more inclined to try to figure out how to keep the meet-

ing on the right track and get the information we need than I am to try to avoid a tense situation."

"You're really going to do this?" demanded Jerry.

"Yep."

"I can't talk you out of making fools of all of us?" he asked hopefully.

"Nope. In fact, I suggest you help me think through how to organize the meeting to diminish your worst nightmares. Planning the meeting carefully would be a lot more effective than trying to talk me out of having a meeting of this kind. If you're right, and the meeting becomes crazy, at least we'll know where we stand. If our customers are out of control with how they feel, we didn't have much of a chance anyway. We might as well start making decisions. The longer we delay, the less we have to work with. We desperately need the whole picture and we need it now."

MORE LESSONS LEARNED

Losing face would cause less fear if you were certain you were making the right decision. Losing confidence in your own judgment is often the result of fear-driven organizations. Learn to improve the odds of making the right choice in fast-moving, unforgiving environments.

How do you improve the odds of getting the solutions right the first time? There are a number of things which are helpful.

Be flexible without being weak! Clarify your vision for the outcome of your decision and incorporate the knowledge and views of others into your vision. When you include the input of others, you increase the odds of finding the best solution. For example, the next time you feel sure that your idea or plan is right, and others disagree, make your response one of trying to figure out how to integrate their idea into yours. Or even better, figure out how to integrate your idea into theirs.

Use your intuition. Close your eyes and imagine all of the steps of the implementation. Play the implementation out in your mind. Identify all of the potential snags. The visualization of implementation of a solution may appear to be an extra step. This extra step will help you to be more thorough in your planning. Often the risky decisions which fail are not due to poor thinking; they are due to poor planning. Get others to imagine symbols that will tell you what things to watch out for and what steps you may need to add to your plan to diminish the impact of the obstacles.

Examine the choice of *not* pursuing the path you believe to be right and try to identify the outcome of not acting. Even if your plan has a risk of failing, if the alternative of not acting leaves you in a worse condition, you have no choice. Knowing you have no choice will give you more confidence.

The last step is to identify where your choice leads you even if the course of action you choose fails. Once you have identified a potential outcome, develop a theory for why the landing place may be a better place from which to take your next steps. If you contemplate how to make a potential failure work *for* you before you take the step, you will diminish your fear of failure. Your confidence improves the likelihood of success. In the chapter on Rhythm, the concept of leveraging obstacles to your advantage was discussed. Leveraging *failures* to your advantage carries the concept further.

The process of gathering information from others, using your intuition, examining the effects of not taking action, and leveraging potential failure before you take action will create better and better solutions. The more good decisions you make, the more likely you are to move more freely next time.

1. Would you describe yourself as flexible? Would others describe you as flexible?

2. Have you made any bad decisions? Identify any positive changes as a result of your bad decision? This might include improved relationships, greater understanding, etc..

3. Use a few words to describe what you would like your image to be in your professional world. Identify a few of the words others would use to describe you.

THINGS TO REMEMBER:

1. **Risk-takers recognize threats as possibilities rather than assuming they are realities. They make their decisions by identifying the potential to do damage in the long-term by not taking the risk. The greater risk is the one with the most potential for becoming real.**

2. **When you are trying to determine a course of action, identify the threats involved in doing what you really want to do. Ask yourself what you would do if those were removed. Then identify how real those threats are and how they stack up against the threat of not doing what you want to do.**

3. **Be sure the reason for a choice is not a fear of losing face. Never allow a fear of losing face to influ-**

ence your decision when trying to determine the best course of action.

PHASE II

CONSISTENCY

Managing Confusion

CONSISTENCY

You are a leader in a corporation. You state what you want. You have been very clear. Increase revenues by x% by the end of the fiscal year. Do so by focusing on .... Why do you hear so many excuses? Why are so many of them based on comments such as, "Our leadership doesn't have a clear sense of direction for this organization."? Consistency is a two edged sword. Your ability to be consistent is related to how consistent you are and how consistent people perceive you to be.

It really does not matter what your role is. As a parent consistency is as much or more of an issue as it is in any corporation. Consistency comes from a core, not from a set of instructions. Your personal and professional power will be affected dramatically by how consistent you are with your core.

People often ask for something different than what they really need. When people say they want direction, often they want to be able to anticipate you and your reactions. They will find security in having a clear understanding of your purpose. They are not just looking for your immediate purpose. They would like a sense of who you are and what you stand for in your totality.

If you are stating your objectives through goals, people may be clear about the outcome you want and still unclear about who you are. 'Are you human? Do you care how we get there? If we are dishonest or take shortcuts to get the result, do you care? What is my value to you as a human being?"

Unfortunately, goals change as the environment exerts its influence. Perhaps the goals you have set are impossible. Soon the environment forces you to change the goals. As the goals change, for example, from 10% to the more realistic 5%, people become confused. Their confidence in you will be undermined. If instead, you consistently stand for some value such as customer focus, integrity, discipline, hard work, etc., you provide a means to the end result. They understand you and they understand where you are unequivocal.

The next three chapters focus on building an understanding of how to create consistency in your style. People's perspective on your consistency is what builds or destroys *trust*.

CHAPTER V

ENGAGEMENT

The first step toward creating consistency is to be totally engaged in your work and ultimately in your life. To be engaged is to be fully alive and vital. To be absolutely engaged is to be unafraid of the truth. To be engaged is to be fully committed to success. Fully committed means you hold nothing back. You do nothing to sabotage your own efforts.

To be engaged is to be aware of yourself. You will constantly battle with your emotions, belief systems, tolerance for risk, and especially with your instincts. You must understand your instincts and their impact on your actions and therefore your results. Often your belief systems, risk tolerance, and emotions are fundamentally driven by the basic need to survive. These elements of your personality go beyond intellect and beyond consciousness.

THE STORY

Debbie came into John's office to share the numbers she had found in her exploration. She had a bemused expression on her face. "I don't know why we didn't see this before," she said. "I guess we were so determined to cut the costs that we lost sight of the big picture. I'm as guilty as anyone."

"What did you find?" asked John. "I thought we might get a surprise."

"Well, first, I wanted to see the whole thing at once.

Last year, when we decided to go after the costs, we really made some progress. Our first and second quarters looked pretty good. I remember how great we felt and we were inspired to cut costs even more. By the fourth quarter we had cut 20% out of our operating budget."

"So, what conclusions did you reach?" asked John with a smile.

"At the time, I thought we were pretty clever and certainly doing our jobs," said Debbie. "But the other side of the picture was our loss of market share became more dramatic. The curve actually became significantly steeper, and by the fourth quarter the result was as if we had cut an artery."

"Do you think there's a connection?" asked John.

"Well, I didn't at first. But then I decided to look at which costs we had made the most significant cuts in and I started to wonder. We cut our advertising budget by 30%. We took our customer service representatives down to 50% and installed answering systems. We switched shipping companies to transport our products, and we engaged in major negotiations with our suppliers, forcing them to take 20 to 25% out of the cost. What's interesting is if you then look at where the majority of our customer complaints come from."

"I thought there might be a connection," said John. "Did you find the complaints focused on delivery, quality, and customer responsiveness?"

"Yes, but we also lost our share of new business. We had been steadily adding new business over the same period the previous year. We added less than 10% of our previous growth."

"I suspect the lack of growth is a reflection of the lack of advertising, but perhaps the slow growth is also is affected by the fact we did not introduce any new products last year. We cut R&D on new products completely out of the budget."

"It is almost as though we had decided to go out of business," said Debbie. "I can't believe we were so shortsighted. All we cared about was that the results showed these huge savings in cost."

"You would probably find Ned's legal information quite supportive of your findings," said John. "There are quite a few issues around shutting down customer lines while they waited for our parts. The worst of it is we stopped listening. We didn't pay attention to the results of our actions. We kept seeing things get worse, but we were so unwilling to acknowledge we might be responsible that we didn't want to see the connections. We found it easier to blame the economic environment or the competition."

"What are we going to do?" asked Debbie.

"Well, we're first going to get on our knees and say thanks that we are starting to understand our own responsibility in this mess. Finding we may be at fault is not pleasant, but before we had this information, all of our problems were blamed on things over which we had no control. We now are back in control. I just hope we haven't been foolish enough to run ourselves out of time. No matter what, one of the hardest things for me to deal with has been the feeling I wouldn't know what to do if I ran into the situation again. I felt worthless as a leader."

"I guess that's looking at the bright side," said Debbie. "But we still need to react now."

"Our first step is to look at the shipping issue. We can get our hands on that one immediately. The quality may be a little more difficult. We will have to work with our suppliers and they're all mad at us because they felt so pressured a year ago during our cost cutting."

"Actually," said Debbie, "while discovering our flaws is a little intimidating, it feels good to have a direction. I've been floundering for so long now. I'm relieved to be swimming again. We dodged our responsibility to manage this business by laying the blame on our suppliers."

THE FUNDAMENTAL

Engagement

Fighting for vitality is often the same as fighting against instinct. Our predisposition to certain types of responses will often create an outcome of pulling back when we should be pushing forward, of disengaging when we should engage, or of detaching when we need to become involved.

Powerful people are engaged. Masterful individuals are aware of and responsive to reality. They are courageous and yet measured and rhythmic in their responses. Our instincts, on the other hand, generally tend to be about surviving and preserving. Personal power and instinct may find many occasions where they work in opposition. Instinct insists we pull back and maintain. Power demands staying involved and expanding.

You are human. At times, your battle to survive may supersede your ability to thrive. You must become aware of the moments where instinct actually works against your ability to stay fully engaged.

SYMPTOMS

There are many symptoms of a lack of engagement. They differ in their severity and potential cost to the individual and the organization.

Individuals who are not engaged often fear bad news. The fear manifests in several ways. This person may operate as the perpetual "good news bear." He or she refuses to acknowledge a serious issue or situation. This person absorbs negative news and re-articulates the negative in a form serving the craving for good news. This is different than leveraging bad news and finding the next step on the path by using it to the good. This is an actual denial of bad news.

Another manifestation of a lack of true engagement is the "kill the messenger" syndrome. This is often not understood as lack of engagement on the part of the "killer," but, in fact, the person who destroys the bearer of bad news is making a very clear statement. He or she is saying, "Do not bring me bad news. I don't want to know!"

More subtle, and possibly more dangerous, symptoms reside within the decisions we make. Decisions of retreat could be expedient initially. Cutting costs, laying off, changing suppliers for lower cost providers, etc. may start as critical decisions for the ongoing health of the organization. These acts of containment become the acts of a disengaged leader when the results these actions generate are a loss of quality in relationships with those who are critical to the success of the business; suppliers, employees, customers, etc.

It is not wrong to pull back and tighten the belt. It *is* wrong to do so as the only strategy. When a person ceases to engage with the environment, he or she will often make shortsighted, withdrawal-oriented decisions.

Identify the decisions to expand which are made simultaneously with those decisions which focus on pulling back. If decisions to grow are not occurring, you are probably disengaging from the act of running the organization. The organization must remain vital and growing even as decisions to leave things behind occur.

LESSONS LEARNED BY POWERFUL PEOPLE

A. The Instinctive Reaction

You have probably learned to trust your instincts. They have, in fact, been a part of your survival. Sometimes your instincts are wrong. Some inherent human reactions to fear may ensure your destruction. When an airplane is stalling, the impulse is to pull back on the stick in order to raise the nose, as if doing so would cause the airplane to go up. Pushing down on the stick to build air speed will save you; pulling back creates a greater stall. When a horse runs away, our instinct is to pull back on the reins with all our might. The horse only fights harder, often creating an instinct in the animal to rear (the most dangerous situation for the rider). When faced by a wild animal, we want to run. The wild animal can often run faster than the person and running simply fuels the animal's instinct to pounce. We run anyway.

People react inappropriately to fear by relying on destructive instincts. We are pulling back when we should be pushing forward. The roots of our fear-based reactions lie in our struggle to preserve, at all costs, what we have.

Examples of this struggle toward preservation are numerous. Companies with massive resources cut back on research, leadership development, and training. Budgets in marketing and sales are attacked when volume drops. Companies install complex answering services, rather than employing people to deal with customers, in order to cut costs. The issue of the customers' feelings about service are irrelevant next to the efficiencies achieved. The same cost issues create the massive use of telemarketing for sales efforts rather than putting real sales people in the field face to face with the customer. All of these actions are examples of acting on the impulse to pull back on the stick when feeling threatened.

Other examples of instincts include the way we deal with the life-blood of our companies when we are afraid. Suppliers and distributors, as well as employees, are handled roughly, and are often perceived as a way of making up the difference in the margins. Cut *their* profits before we cut our own!

At a personal level, the instincts are the same. It seems the more a person has to lose, the greater the instinct to conserve. People with relatively large resources will often react more protectively than people of lesser means. They may not react at all for a long time when the problems are obvious to all, and then they really pull back on the reins when they realize things are out of control. The challenge is to know the difference between a pragmatic decision and a destructive, fear-based reaction. *And* to understand the costs.

Staying engaged means staying in the battle, not withdrawing. You must stay informed. Do not demand people give you the answer you want to hear. Staying engaged means taking the risk of knowing the truth about yourself, your organization, and the environment. Knowing when to push forward rather than pull back is critical.

B. Scarcity vs. Abundance

Lack of engagement is a behavior that grows over time. The roots of the behavior lie in a philosophy. The philosophy behind the behavior is "scarcity". We are never convinced there is more abundance than we can consume. We are *invariably* afraid there is not enough. We have conviction that if we do not take whatever we want first, someone else will take our desire away from us. We operate from greed because we know everyone else does. Instinct takes over and we "survive".

We are afraid if we lose our job, there may not be another. If we spend our last resources on what may not work, we will cease to exist! We operate as if our job is truly in jeopardy. We are afraid of what lies around the corner if what lies around the corner is unlike the road we are on.

Our fears may be accurate! The reality of our fear is what makes managing instinctive response so difficult. The instinct was developed for a reason. Unfortunately, if we do not find ways to expand rather than contract, our fears will probably manifest into reality. The challenge is to let go of fear, trust in ourselves, and create rather than destroy.

It is not easy to face a potential ending. Many of us have built our own sense of self-worth around our success. Our instinctive reactions are to clutch at what we have, rather than to let go and re-evaluate who we are and what we could be instead. We hate change because we are afraid of the unknown. We somehow assume the change will lessen us. This becomes reality in the corporate world manifesting as continuous downsizing without innovation.

ASK YOURSELF

1. Is your organization's instinct to become more aggressive or to withdraw when faced with crisis? Examine issues like what happens to the way you spend money, where are dollars added and where are they withdrawn, etc.?

2. Is your personal pattern to become more aggressive or to withdraw when faced with a crisis? Remember to examine your overall patterns rather than a few instances of aggression or withdrawal. For example, when you feel as though your career is in jeopardy, do you become more loose and free with your decision-making style, or more

constrained? Do you 'go for broke' or become cautious?

3. Can you imagine asking for feedback from your peers around your decision-making, relationship skills, ego, etc. Note: this is not a survey form which is distributed and returned anonymously. This question refers to a direct interaction and engagement with their feelings about you.

MORE LESSONS LEARNED

A. Disengage From the Need for Security

The response to tough times should be bold. You must be unafraid to know the worst and to engage joyfully in the battle. Examine your instincts. Embrace them for their value in survival, and then *choose* not to be captive to them.

This book is not written for the easy, lush times. *What To Do When It Rains* is intended to challenge you to do something different during the tough times when none of the decisions are obvious. You may need to spend *more* of your limited resources, not less, in tough times. If you know intuitively you are creating a rather long and slow death, why not 'flame out'?

Try to think in terms of, "If I know the current path I am on is likely to get smaller and smaller, why not take what I have and go for broke?"

Find a way to act as if you have nothing to lose. If you are downsizing, and you are going to do more downsizing, you should spend money. Do not just accept more and more limits as an outcome! You will have *less* resources to save yourself the longer you stay on the path of retreat. Act aggressively now when the curve is not so steep.

If you are afraid of running out of something, personally or professionally, you will *never* have enough to make you feel secure. You will just keep increasing the amount you need to make you feel safe. We have built a culture on this philosophy. And the culture is letting us down. We are actually creating less and less security.

There is no security! Your future resides in your ability to accept this truth. When you know and accept security as an illusion, you will more easily make the choice to push down on the stick rather than pull up when the airplane is stalling.

The paradox is that *then, and only then,* you will ensure your security. You will do the right thing in the right moment, rather than try to protect something which does not exist! The only way to create this change in attitude is to have more faith in yourself and the universe. Believe, if you try and fail, that the learning was worth the risk.

When you imagine pursuing an aggressive, risky course of action you may think of others for whom you are responsible. Your caution and lack of risk-taking may leave them disappointed in the long run. Challenge yourself to stay balanced between risk-taking and security. To do so may mean pushing yourself to take risks beyond your comfort zone.

There are broader implications to becoming more comfortable with risk. If as a society, we are making our personal choices not to take risks, then we may be teaching our children to clutch rather than to believe in themselves. Often, they become our excuse for not trying and risking. Personal obligations are the most often cited rationales for reluctance to do the right thing if there is a security risk attached

1. Are you operating in a manner you would call bold to day? Would others call it bold?

2. Are your organization's strategic plans for the future bold or cautious? Are there things that could be changed making the strategies more bold? Should those changes be made?

3. Is your organization pulling back on the stick symbolically right now? Describe the crash that is likely to occur if it continues to pull back. Are you pulling back on the stick symbolically in any way? Describe the crash that may occur if you do not change?

THINGS TO REMEMBER:

1. **Dare yourself to do more. Invest in people, product, and promotion when all your instincts scream at you to pull back.**

2. **Imagine how your customers feel about you. Do the right thing no matter what!**

3. **Do not cut research. Use your research dollars more efficiently.**

4. **Pretend you *knew* you were going out of business if you did not react appropriately. What would you do differently?**

5. **Respond to all of the above statements personally as well.**

CHAPTER VI

RESPONSIVENESS

The quality of responsiveness in a person reflects a sensitivity and an ability to react appropriately to the environment. A leader preparing to take greater and greater risks must be certain he or she is taking the right risks.

The only way to determine whether a leader is taking risks successfully is to examine results. Responsiveness (*productive* responsiveness) is based on your ability to observe and understand the law of cause and effect.

THE STORY

John, Jerry, and Debbie were meeting about the results of the cost studies. Jerry was happy with the conclusions reached by John and Debbie.

"I don't believe our loss of market share is related to our cost cutting. That's too big a leap for me. I don't know how you could ever prove such a thing."

"Well, let's look at it this way," suggested John. "What were we thinking in terms of our customers when we made the decisions?"

"We weren't thinking in terms of our customers at the time," Jerry said angrily. "We were thinking in terms of survival."

"Exactly," said John. "We weren't thinking in terms of

our customers, and we made decisions reflecting lack of concern for their requirements. As a result, they are telling us in a multitude of ways we have been thoughtless where their needs are concerned."

"Well, we have to take care of ourselves first," said Jerry. "If we don't, I can't see how we're going to be able to take care of them in the future."

"I guess the thing becoming clear to me is I've been way too focused on taking care of myself," said John. "I've made all these decisions to look good in the short-term, and I did look good in the *short-term*. Ironically, with all my focus on the short-term, looking good is getting more and more elusive in any term."

"I have no idea what you are trying to accomplish," said Jerry with venom. "You are really operating in la-la land these days. I can't even relate to what you say anymore."

Debbie spoke up at this point. "You know, Jerry, John really does have a point. Two weeks ago we were all desperately trying to figure out what to do next. Nothing was working. We weren't in la-la land, but we weren't getting anywhere either. Since we've been trying to figure out how to create the larger picture, I've seen lots more clarity in our thinking. We're getting clearer answers from our customers about what's wrong. We're seeing the connection of our results to our thinking. Focusing on our results helps us to focus on where to start."

"I'm also feeling a lot better these days," said John, "for the very reasons Debbie is talking about. I feel as though I have a direction again. I'm seeing the outcomes surrounding me as results of how I've been thinking about the issues. I feel really good knowing I'm in a position of control again. I'm really looking forward to our meeting with customers and employees tomorrow. I think then we'll all need to sit down and do some real strategic thinking about our future. Once we have the information, we have a chance to be responsive."

"I think this is all nonsense," said Jerry. "I think we're going to get in there and they're going to tear us apart. We'll be no better off then we were before, but we'll have lost any credibility we still had."

"You may be right," said John. "But I'm willing to take the risk. I don't know any other way to convince our customers we are really committed to solving our problems. They've listened to the words long enough. They don't believe us any more. We will have to take more risks than this meeting to get Sorot turned around. By the way, you should know I've invited a few of our major suppliers."

"I should have guessed," said Jerry, throwing his hands up in the air. "Now all our enemies are invited to the party. Perhaps you should have invited the bankers as well. Let's strip in front of everybody who counts."

There was a gleam in John's eye. "What an interesting suggestion. I should have thought of the bankers myself."

"Oh, no!" Jerry wailed. "I'll learn to keep my mouth shut."

Debbie was thoughtful. "I wonder when we began to think of our customers, suppliers and employees as enemies?" she said as she left the room.

◆ ◆ ◆ ◆ ◆ ◆

THE FUNDAMENTAL

Responsiveness

The ability to respond appropriately to situations depends to a great degree on your ability to analyze the outcomes you create. The most important factor for analysis utilizes a slightly modified version of the physical concept of the law of cause and effect. For every action there is a reaction. *Cause* is the decision or action starting *effects* in motion.

Can you clearly identify, for every element of your current reality, the cause which set the effects in motion? The ability to do so is critical to the choices you will make next. If you do not develop an almost spiritual understanding of cause and effect, you may never understand the events and choices creating ongoing crisis in your personal and professional life. You will repeat the same quality of results with your choices until you do.

SYMPTOMS

The first and most obvious clue if you are not responsive to the law of cause and effect in your choices is repetitive crisis. If you find similar, repetitive patterns in your crises, there is something you are not paying attention to.

For example, do you constantly run into money/budget problems? You may find that you blame problems on outside events or circumstances, but if it happens in a reoccurring paradigm, it is likely there is an element of how you think about budget which must be examined.

If there is a pattern to the types of disagreements you have with others, there is a causal relationship at work. Identifying the cause of the patterns is not easy, especially if the pattern has been with you for a long time.

There are many symptoms of causal relationships gone bad. Basically any situation operating in a state of chaos is the result of chaotic thinking. You must look around you and determine what is not working. Ask yourself a series of basic questions that start with, "How did I create this reality?" and "Why did I create this?"

This set of questions is appropriate even with events appearing outside of your control. For example, if the chaos is within your company or client companies and you are affected by the turmoil which is part of a cultural pattern, why are you choosing to be a part of it? What choices could you make to stop the chaos? What risks have you been unwilling to take? The price you are now paying is always a reflection of your choices.

LESSONS LEARNED BY POWERFUL PEOPLE

Most people recognize, but pay little attention in their *professional* life to, the old saying "What goes around comes around." We operate our lives, our businesses and our organizations around a different set of laws. The focus usually is on *results*, and results are measured in money, power, and advancement.

Often, because you are so focused on these most visible signs of success, you may remain oblivious and therefore unresponsive to the more subtle clues that will tell you what to do next. While money, power, and advancement are symptoms of your success, they are often symptoms that lag behind the reality creating the next set of results.

The law of cause and effect is one of equality of energy and results. Whatever energy has been put into the system is always returned. The choices you make now will manifest in outcomes later. If you are to be effective in your leadership or in your life, you must be prepared to evaluate the past in terms of how you and others were thinking at the time.

If you think and plan for scarcity, you will find scarcity. If you think in terms of using people to achieve your ends, people will feel used. If you have made many short-term decisions to gain momentum on the bottom line, decisions not necessarily good for the long-term health of the company, you will quite likely experience very short-term payoffs for your actions. You will find yourself in a cycle of continually having to come up with the next short-term gimmick to stay ahead with your customers.

For example, suppose you are not getting ahead financially in the way you desire. As you look at your career choices in the past, how many of them were heavily influenced by the amount of money you were paid for the move? While you were paid accordingly in the short-term, you may have made the very decision that put a *cap* on your income. If you examine some of your past decisions now, can you find ways that they have limited your growth personally? If you based your decision on making a certain amount of money, you are now making a *certain* amount of money.

If you make decisions based on getting visibility, you will get visibility. You may get the wrong kind of visibility or become noticed for your mistakes rather than your accomplishments. In everything you do examine the direct relationship between the outcome you create and what you were thinking you wanted at the time you made the decision.

ASK YOURSELF

1. Are you satisfied with your current income? What are some of the choices you have made that have created this income? What are some of the risks you have avoided that have created this income? What are some of the risks you have avoided that may have capped your income?

2. What patterns do you see in your current relationships? Look at the bad relationships and determine what they have in common, and then do the same for the good relationships.

3. What are some of the basic patterns in your life and what have you done to create them? Do you like them? What would you have done differently?

MORE LESSONS LEARNED

Making Cause and Effect Work for You

There is a common expression useful in working with cause and effect: "Intention equals results." Imagine that intentions literally do equal results. The results you see are the results you intended. If you change your intention, you can change the results.

The first step is to make sure you are thinking in complete terms about what you want to create. If you are trying to be noticed for being "good" in your organization, be sure you really think through what "good" is. Complete your vision. Is "good" just smart or sharp? Do you want to be known for short-term results or long-term shrewdness and vision, or both? If you frame the way you are thinking about what you want more completely, you will make different decisions obtaining different outcomes.

For example, if you want to make a certain amount of money, ask yourself why. If the answer is you want to stop worrying about money, then frame your desire to say, "I want to stop worrying about money." Otherwise, your cause or motive is limited. Your desire becomes focused on an amount rather than a feeling. You may create, eventually, what you want but by the time you do, you will probably have increased your expenses enough in the meantime to continue to feel the need to worry.

If you make your goal a feeling of financial security, the goal may still be too limited. Think in terms of having more money than you can possibly use, while at the same time you think about doing something you love intensely. The very framing in your mind becomes more complete. Perhaps you would like to add an objective of living somewhere you love, or near people you love. Thinking in complete terms about what you want will dramatically change some of the choices producing limited results.

You may accept a job which offers less income initially because you need to learn certain skills that will enable you to run your own business in the future. You may take work allowing you more flexibility in terms of where you live. Do not get locked in to any one facet of what you desire or you will create a narrow outcome.

In your business or organizational decisions, be sure you create a complete picture of the outcome before you make a decision to improve a product line or increase business. Include assertions indicating how each conclusion impacts long-term revenue as well as short-term results. How does each choice fit into the overall plan and vision, including how the choice impacts employees and suppliers as well as customers?

There are two messages regarding the law of cause and effect. The first is to only "put out" what you wish to receive. If you create dead bodies in the process of achieving your ambitions, you will ultimately become a dead body. The second is to bring greater quality into your decision-making process by realizing your results are an outcome of the quality of the original decisions. If you feel what you have achieved is not enough, then you did not think broadly enough about what you wanted to construct in the first place.

ASK YOURSELF

1. What are some of the things that have gone wrong in your life? If you acknowledge that intentions equal results worked for those things, what do you feel?

2. Why are you intending things that are clearly causing you discomfort? What are you learning or gaining from the discomfort that you need to learn?

3. Think of something you really want and have wanted for a long time. Is there some reason you may be holding back from attaining it?

THINGS TO REMEMBER:

1. **For any crisis, there is a causal relationship to decisions made in the past. You must understand the cause to solve the problem.**

2. **For any unhappy element in your life, you have made a decision to create the circumstances making you unhappy. Identify the decision.**

3. **Each time you make a decision, ask what the long-term implications of the decision might be!**

4. **The people you influence will trust you only if you truly understand your accountability to outcomes.**

CHAPTER VII

DIRECTION

An individual's sense of direction, both personal and professional, is the next most important understanding to be developed. Often this sense of direction is interpreted as, "What market should we go after?" or "Where shall we allocate our resources?". Those questions are premature if you have not done the demanding work of defining your presence in the context of a larger purpose.

Do you know your larger purpose? Can you look at yourself and say, "This is what I'm about and clearly I'm here to contribute........?" This larger purpose is not a part of a job description. You are seeking a spiritual knowing of the fundamental characteristic of your being and its purpose.

An understanding of your spiritual uniqueness and your contribution will help you make more consistent decisions. If you know, for example, one of your most fundamental characteristics is to provide logic in chaotic situations, when faced with a crisis, you will more quickly identify what logic is needed and you will express your decision as a form of logic. Soon others will turn to you for what you have consistently delivered. If you have not defined yourself or your organization in terms of essence and your contribution to a larger purpose, you or the organization will flounder each time the wind changes.

THE STORY

John was lost in thought. He had seen so much of what motivated people in the last few days. There was nothing like crisis to identify people's vulnerabilities. As he reflected on what he was learning, he began to see a pattern. He began to comprehend integral pieces to being able to retake control of the situation. He had needed to work through panic and the fear of failure. He would never have gotten beyond the fear if he had not taken the walk in the park before the board meeting and realized how important relaxation was to his ability to let go of his ego.

There were so many things he now understood. Most importantly, he understood his responsibility as a leader to examine the results of his choices. And yet, he was stuck. He did not know what to do next. He had so much information, and still the next steps were unclear.

Jackie came in and handed him a letter to be signed. "You look gloomy again. I haven't seen you look this way for weeks."

"I am. I probably shouldn't be, but I am."

"Well, what do you need to feel better?" Jackie asked with genuine concern.

"I guess I need to know what this is all for," John said despondently. He thought about what he had said and grinned. "No little question I've asked you to wrestle with, is it? Even if we fix everything wrong, so what? Do we just exist for the next crisis? It all seems meaningless to me."

"There is always a purpose for everything, even hard times," Jackie said. "We've certainly seen some of those. I think maybe you're asking the wrong question."

"What do you mean?" Jackie had such a gift for making him feel better. She always saw right through the swirling debris and focused on the question making things clear.

"Well, instead of asking what the meaning of all this is, why don't you ask what your purpose is? I read a book called *One* by Richard Bach saying something like, 'I gave my whole life to become who I am. Was it worth it?'"

"Say more," said John with interest. "I'm not sure where you're going, but the direction feels right."

"What if you knew you had been in training your whole life just to help this corporation and its people see things differently? What are the things you have learned or done that make you exactly the right person for this now?"

"You're really asking me to think about who I am."

"I guess so," she said. "It seems to me everyone has a unique essence. The essence is the magic each person has to contribute."

" I guess," she continued, "you are looking for the 'why.' After your work a few weeks ago, you have a sense of the organization you are trying to create. Now you are asking, 'So what?' You need to figure out why you are the only person who can get this organization back on track. What is your role?"

"I'm not sure I'm the only one who can help the organization," said John, somewhat awkwardly.

"I am," said Jackie. "And you happen to be in charge. So you have to."

"If only it were so simple," John replied, shaking his head.

"That's the point!" Jackie said with passion.

John looked at her with surprise. She was usually so low-keyed.

"It *is* simple. You make everything so complex. I believe you and every person involved have a specific gift to give to this effort. If you stop trying to figure it all out and just focus on what you each do best, I think the solutions will become clear."

John knew better than to argue. There was something about her passion causing him not to question the practical nature of her words. Instead he tried to focus on his essence.

"I assume you're looking for a fundamental quality about me that pervades everything I am?" he suggested.

"Exactly."

"I guess the one thing I think I'm really about is honesty."

"Yes, but you're honest in a particular way. You look at yourself and you are willing to admit when you are wrong. Sometimes I don't think you have an ego."

"I assure you I have an ego," said John laughing. He got up and started walking around the large office, looking at the things on his walls and the memorabilia spread around the room. In a way, he was trying to trace his path to this moment in time by looking at everything important from his career. There were awards from special projects, there were the pictures with politicians, and there were numerous mementos from various seminars and events. As he looked at the tangible evidence of his journey, he realized how important his ability to be honest with himself and others had been. Each time a project had stalled, he had looked within for the faulty thinking. He always found the next step through an ability to let go of his ego and find where he might have gone wrong.

"You know, Jackie, you may be right. I really have used the ability to question myself to get through difficult times. This is really no different, except the stakes are higher."

"If that's your gift, then you need to do it now. But you might also think about making the whole organization claim the ability to look honestly at itself as your gift to the organization. Then the solution is lasting as opposed to another win for John Dobbs."

"You certainly give me lots to think about. The first thing

is to frame the meeting tomorrow around an attitude of an organization looking inward for the flaws in its thinking."

As Jackie left the room, John wondered about her. She was so wise and yet she had so little ambition. They had had many conversations about what she wanted from her career. Her response was always the same. She was content right where she was. "Perhaps her lack of ambition has something to do with her essence," John thought to himself. "Perhaps she gets her meaning in life from helping people like me."

John spent a lot of time over the next hours thinking about the concept of essence and what the concept could mean to him and his team.

◆ ◆ ◆ ◆ ◆ ◆

THE FUNDAMENTAL

Direction

Every organization and every leader is faced with an almost unlimited number of options in decision-making. There are times when this multitude of options is not evident, but the choices still exist. The role of the leader and for that matter, every individual, is to make choices.

All the choices you make reflect a direction. When examined in their entirety, your choices will reflect who you are. If your decisions lack the understandings of the previous chapters, they may reflect insecurity, risk-aversion, and a lack of observance of the laws of cause and effect.

Imagine you have mastered the understandings of the previous chapters and have built a legacy of good decisions with positive and productive results. You are still incomplete. As you evolved you have been learning things about yourself. There are patterns helping you understand your uniqueness as a human being.

You may be a good decision-maker but your real contribution is your uniqueness. *Every* leader and every powerful person, must know his or her unique essence and find ways to make the essence clear with every decision. This clarity helps the leader set a definite direction for his or her organization. This clarity of purpose creates the consistencies causing others to trust and then follow. Without this clarity, others will be less likely to entrust you with their energies, their futures, and their vulnerabilities.

For example, John's essence is the search for and confrontation of truth. He has not made this clear, either by expressing his essence daily in his choices, or insisting his team live the essence of doing the right thing as an expression of each of their individual choices.

Imagine John had been more aware of his essence. How would his leadership team have operated differently? How much of the present crisis could have been alleviated through consistent pursuit of truth?

Another example might be helpful. What if John's essence was different than truth seeker? Would the organization still find a path within the alternative essence? The answer is yes. Suppose John had discovered in his essence a unique ability to nurture and care about people. Without a recognition and application of this essence in his decision-making, the results would have been similar to what we are seeing in the story.

If he had chosen to live an essence of caring and nurturing, his team might have been forced to confront some of its own self-serving, non-caring attitudes. By focusing on creating a sensitive and empathetic organization, John might have created an organization perceived by customers and employees alike as caring and nurturing.

His essence is the stamp he must now place on the organization. You, too, must know your essence and factor the knowledge into your decisions. If you do not express your essence through your choices, your decisions will not seem to follow any predictable pattern. Because your family, peers, employees or customers want to figure you out, they may attribute inaccurate motives to your decisions.

SYMPTOMS

The first symptom of a lack of clarity of personal purpose or direction is created by your response to the following question: Do you know your essence? Can you identify in one word what the most fundamental quality of your personality and spirit is? If you can not, others will not be able to clearly identify who you are either.

Symptoms of a lack of clarity of purpose often manifest in issues of trust. People describe you in terms that seem unfamiliar and also uncomfortable. Often they speak of not trusting your motives, thinking you are cold when you think you are warm and caring, etc.. Others might attribute your decisions to your ambition. If people perceive ambition as opposed to truth or caring as your motive, they do so because you have allowed them to doubt your motives through your own erratic behaviors.

If you are often stuck for the right answer, you have not done the work to determine your essence. The answer to impasse always lies within your essence. If you do not know what to do, do something reflecting who you are! You will often face decisions with multiple options. For example, John had infinite options facing him. He did not know where to focus. By utilizing the dimension of "honesty," he clarifies himself to his organization. He focuses his energy on the search for truth.

If John's essence had been nurturing instead of honesty, his choice might have been to focus his energy on creating a nurturing organization. It does not matter what the essence is. What is important is the clarity and the impact of the clarity.

Another symptom of a lack of direction on your part is confusion in others. If those you influence have a difficult time predicting you, and find themselves indecisive where you are concerned, they do not have a clear sense of what is important to you. There is a lack of clarity in your cumulative decisions making you unpredictable.

LESSONS LEARNED BY POWERFUL PEOPLE

Setting personal and organizational direction is even harder today than it was a few years ago. We confused leaders dramatically with all of the misunderstandings around the application of teams and employee involvement programs. Does employee involvement mean abdication of responsibility of the leader? Do teams mean a lack of recognition of the *individual's* potential and accountability?

Many people became tentative because to be forceful about setting direction might have appeared to be a lack of willingness to be part of the team. Anyone making an independent decision without consulting the team appears arrogant. The role of the leader needs to be redefined in the cooperative environment where empowering employees is included in the design of the organization. Unfortunately, as we rushed to create employee involvement programs, the role of the leader was often neglected.

Employee involvement is not a fad. It is in an important facet of our evolution. However, we are far from a complete understanding of the leader's role within these cultures. Ideally, as you learn to understand and apply your own unique contribution to the whole, you will become better at recognizing the uniqueness of others. Employee involvement will happen because you cannot imagine decisions occurring any other way.

A person may choose to believe the universe has placed exactly the right people with exactly the right unique skill or talent to contribute in every situation. John can embrace the potential contribution of others while still being very demanding regarding the search for truth.

A. Determining Personal Essence

Determining essence is not easy. Your essence is that quality which fundamentally describes who you are. Find your essence by examining what you have done in significant moments in your life. You are searching for those moments when you were operating at your most powerful and when you had enormous success as a result.

Within those moments are the clues. How did you make the success happen? Are you a wonderful problem-solver? Are you great at managing personal relationships and motivating others? Are you caring and nurturing? Are you honest?

Examine whatever comes to mind when you ask yourself what you are most proud of in your life. The moment of your greatest personal power is not always work-related. You may think of having been happily married for thirty years as a great accomplishment. Determine what deep part of your character made the longevity of the marriage possible.

Within this information is a quality you possess which will pervade all of your choices. If you are married happily for thirty years because of your ability to listen, compromise, empathize, etc., do the people you work with perceive these qualities? Do you demonstrate these qualities with all of your decisions?

If, for some reason, you do not believe you should share this side of yourself with others, you are distorting something fundamentally you. A woman engineer at a Fortune 100 company described herself as caring and nurturing when asked about her essence. When she was asked whether her peers would recognize this quality in her, she responded, "Oh, no. A woman can not show that part of herself in corporate life. People will think she's a pushover."

This is a very powerful example of the cost of leaving your essence out of your choices. This woman was very conflicted with bad working relationships. Others did not trust her motives because she was not being herself. As a result of her discovery, she gave herself permission to exhibit more of her essence at work. Immediately she began to get more recognition. People were more willing to share praise easily because her relationships became more cooperative. She allowed herself to share more empathy for their constraints and they in turn felt safer with her.

Do you know your essence? Have you thought about how you might live your essence continuously? Do you understand how your performance and psychological well-being is affected when others do not value your essence?

1. Are others clear about your core essence? Why or why not?

2. Do you consciously make decisions which consistently reflect who you are at a fundamental level? Could you or others describe this in one word?

3. Are you able to translate who you are at home into who you are at work? Could others or would they describe you as different at home than you are at work?

MORE LESSONS LEARNED

B. Does the Organization Know Its Essence?

The next understanding necessary in order to be more effective as a leader and an individual is an understanding of group vision. The leader must evolve the right vision for his or her organization. The parent must evolve the right vision for the family. The organization's vision should also reach for the essence, or the heart, of the organization. The leader must ask what the organization has to contribute to the world. What is the organization's unique gift to give? A family vision might be simpler and yet more profound. What do you want this family's essence to be. What do you want it's members to stand for?

You may *feel* you have created a vision for your organization or your family, but the test comes in the implementation. For *every* decision made, do people ask if the decision supports the vision? As a rule, Americans tend to be very goal-driven. Our own and our organization's essence is often undermined by our short-term need to focus on a goal. Many organizations do the work of creating a vision and then set goals acting in direct opposition to the vision.

For example, if a company decides to be the best in customer service, and then sets a goal for growth that stretches the organization beyond its ability to give the kind of service customers really want, decisions will have to be made to determine how to manage the growth in a way that supports the vision. The organization may need to slow down the growth until systems are put in place to make the growth work in cooperation with a vision of customer service. If people are not managing the growth in terms of the vision, the vision becomes worthless.

If you have been taught to focus on a goal, ask yourself if the goals you are setting are in sync with who you want to be as a person and how you want to be known. Goals can be used to help reach vision, or they can become a short-term focus for what we think we *should* want.

If you become driven by wants, quality of life will fall away from you. Situations will develop which will reflect the choices you have made. You will find yourself uneasy and dissatisfied, even when you have what you thought you wanted.

What is true for individual leaders is true for organizational personalities as well. If you lead an organization away from its essence the organization will falter and create a multitude of unhealthy symptoms to encourage you to steer back to the right path.

ASK YOURSELF

1. What is your essence in one word? Note: essence al
ways denotes a fundamental positive quality at the
core of your identity. What is your group's essence?
This could be your family or your organization.

2. Do you take every opportunity to define yourself clearly
to the world? Do you define your organization to the world
regularly?

3. Are there actions you could take that would help others
see your essence more clearly?

MORE LESSONS LEARNED

C. Making Vision Practical!

Practical is more than dollars and cents. For the purpose of
the following discussion, think of the organization as either a business entity or any entity where you feel a responsibility. Organization can represent a church group, a family, or any connected
group of individuals where you exert an influence. Ultimately, powerful people operate as leaders of others, whether they have consciously chosen to do so, or not.

Leaders have as much responsibility to create *emotionally*
healthy organizations as they do to create *financially* healthy organizations. Individuals have as much responsibility to create emotionally healthy families as they do to create financially healthy
families. Unfortunately, with the enormous pressure on you to be
responsive to the financial demands, you may struggle to see the
emotional side of running a business, or a family, as being equally
relevant.

If an organization is thriving financially, but dying in its essence, the financial picture will eventually begin to falter. People who are not allowed to live their essence will find other rewards, usually at the expense of the organization. Family members will make choices to fill the empty spaces within them that may ultimately be self-destructive, no matter how financially secure they are. Employees will find ways to act out against the unresponsive organization.

Creativity and energy in the organization will diminish if the organizational essence is lost, just as you would lose creativity and energy if you lost your essence. Reinventing comes from creativity, not from forced structural changes. Healthy, vibrant organizations will continue to thrive financially. Consider when your organization was operating at a peak. What was the energy like? How did people feel about their work? How did family members feel about the family? Which came first, the healthy group entity or the financial reward? Does it matter? The two concepts rely on each other in order for the organization to thrive.

If you are at a loss how to create the financial rewards for yourself or for the organization, focus on helping the organization live the essence. If you are focusing on the financial rewards at the *expense* of the organization's essence or at the expense of the essence of the individuals (ultimately they are one and the same), any financial gain will be short-lived.

As a leader (any person desiring to attain personal power becomes a leader), you are responsible for offering a model of leadership focusing on living your essence and in making sure you are demanding the same of the organization, whether it be a family or a company. Imagine all of the decisions you have made in the last month compared against this model. Do they begin to change shape and clarify? Do you have the courage to trust yourself enough to make your choices based on such a model?

Being focused on helping the organization live its essence means when you decide what market to enter, or what new product to support, or where to live, or what job to take, you are making choices that enhance the organization's essence, *as well as* the ones which will make the most money in the short-term. You are making choices for the long term, not the short term. You are unafraid to make unpopular decisions because you know they are right.

You hire people based on their credentials as well as their ability to portray their essence through their choices. The criteria for the right decisions are enlarged to include the essence. You do not have the right answer until you have created one which includes the organization's essence and the essence of the individuals.

When you are determining where to allocate resources, or how to reorganize, you focus on what will create the most opportunity to enhance the organization's essence. The decisions reflect the essence you want people to comprehend.

To live essence takes great courage. You might have to make tough decisions in order to stay true to a vision which includes living the essence. If you are challenging yourself to be the highest form of leader, ultimately you will have to make this leap. Living your essence is similar to jumping off a cliff when you do not know what is below. You have to develop faith, even if you land badly. The decisions will become more fluid as you learn to trust how much better you feel when you follow through with your essence as well as the essence of the group.

1. Do you remember a time in your career or your per
    sonal life where you struggled to make sense of why
    you were there and what you were getting from the
    situation? Can you identify ways in which the issues
    may have been about your core essence?

2. What happened to your energy, motivation, and commit-
    ment at the time?

3. Do you have anyone under you who seems to be a misfit
    for the position? Is it possible that you are asking for an
    execution of the job function which is not in sync with the
    person's essence? Could you find a way to execute the
    responsibilities of the position through a better use of what
    was core to this person's essence? Could you be asking
    something of a family member that is in discord with his or
    her personal essence?

4. Now look at your entire team. Identify, through interac-
    tion and dialogue, the essence of every member of the
    team. Strip away job descriptions, and your own beliefs
    about what makes success, and imagine everyone living
    fully and vitally what they are most perfectly designed to
    do.

THINGS TO REMEMBER:

1. **Use your essence to determine the immediate steps
    you need to take to change your organization for
    the better.**

2. **Identify the essence of the others you influence and
    help them find a way to apply their essence.**

3. Examine the history of the organization to deter mine the essence of the organization and use this knowledge to determine the best course of action.

PHASE III

POWER

Managing Arrogance

POWER

Power is the ultimate objective of anyone who accepts the responsibility of personal mastery. Power comes in many forms. Positional power is acquired through placement. Positional power does not guarantee cooperation and results. Nor does the lack of positional power indicate a lack of personal power.

Your training may have prepared you to believe your status and position give you certain advantages by right. To obtain true personal power, you must understand the inappropriateness of using position or status to feed the ego. Attitudes around position or status rarely enhance a person's personal power. Personal power is achieved only through the evolution of a healthy ego. A healthy ego is only achieved through the absence of arrogance.

CHAPTER VIII

BALANCE

A balanced person is able to stay calm and adaptable in crisis situations. Turning on a dime when things are not working to head in another direction, all the while making people feel relaxed and fearless, is a sign the individual has learned the art of balance.

We often underestimate the potential of a crisis to throw us off balance. How do we know when we have entered into a time of crisis, personally, professionally, or organizationally? And how can we respond to crisis in a way which leaves us and the organization steady and poised for the next leap forward?

THE STORY

John leaned comfortably against the wall of the building talking to Jerry. His demeanor was calm and peaceful. Jerry, on the other hand, was quite agitated. He was pacing and throwing his hands in the air in frustration as he tried to convince John he was on the wrong path.

"We have got to do something tangible now!" he said with anger. "All of this processing is driving me crazy. We need to take some kind of action."

"What do you suggest?" asked John.

"We need to let some of these lead weights around here go. We need to make a statement."

"Just what kind of statement are you trying to make?" asked John.

"We must take this seriously. If we don't take action, the stockholders will assume we think everything is fine."

"I have a hard time imagining how anyone could think everything was fine," responded John. "You always try to find someone to blame for the problem. Who would you suggest?"

"We've had this conversation. You *know* what I think. I really don't know how to convince you our clients need to see some blood. How else will they take us seriously?"

"Jerry, I think I understand where you're coming from," said John. "I think you're as frustrated as the rest of us. And you're afraid because this is the first time in your career you haven't been able to figure out the answers. When life is like that, you just want the solutions to be clear. If only the answer was as easy as finding the right person to blame then we could get on with business. Right?"

"I don't know," said Jerry, quieting somewhat. AI keep thinking this nightmare will end and we can get back to doing our jobs."

"I don't think the solutions are so easy," said John. AI think we're being tested. If we want to get through this, we'll have to pull together, not segment right now. I also think you might find some of the answers if you were to examine your worst fears about this. I know I've gone through some interesting things," he continued.

"Like what ?@ asked Jerry curiously. "You seem so calm and the sky is literally falling on us."

"I realized I was burned out. I had become numb from all the stress. It was hard to make any decision and every task seemed overwhelming. I stopped having fun a long time ago."

"What did you do?" asked Jerry. "You seem so detached now."

"I finally asked myself why I was feeling so ambivalent. I realized I could eliminate the ambivalence if I let go of trying to please everybody. I needed the freedom to move the way I wanted to move with the decisions we were making around here. I had completely lost my sense of self."

"Are you suggesting I've lost my sense of self?" asked Jerry testily.

"I'm suggesting your issues might be even worse," said John, not unkindly. "I think you may be so frightened of the potential fallout from this crisis in terms of your personal and professional life that you are looking for any way to escape, including the destruction of your peers."

Jerry stood very still. He was left speechless by John's bluntness and yet Jerry knew he had been quite vocal about finding a scapegoat. The honesty was what left him with no retort. What could he possibly say? That John's accusation was untrue? He *had* blamed his peers. And there was not much he could say about John's interpretation. At least John had made him seem less diabolical by determining he was doing the blaming because of his panic. He appeared as a balloon that was slowly deflating in front of John's eyes.

"I guess I have been a little crazy lately. I've lost my sense of balance through this thing. Any suggestions?"

"I think we all need to take a deep breath and ask ourselves what would make this feel better. Then we need to support each other and just go through the steps, no matter where the path takes us. Who knows? If our efforts don't turn out the way we want maybe I could open the sporting goods store I've wanted for years. What would you do if this all suddenly went away?"

"I never really thought about what else I would do. I guess I've always wanted to be a consultant. I watch those guys and I think what fun if I were able to go into any business and look at the problems with the detachment of an outsider."

"In some ways, maybe this whole thing is preparing you to gain the perspective of an outsider," said John. "If we can learn to handle our fear and pull together now, what we learn from doing so will make us all more solid for our next adventure, no matter what happens."

"I need to think about all this," said Jerry. "I'm afraid I haven't been introspective in a long time. I guess I never had much use for exploring all my thoughts and emotions. I thought self-analysis was for people who were running to their therapists all the time."

John smiled to himself as Jerry walked to his car. Perhaps Jackie had been right again. His role here was to help everybody be honest with themselves as they worked through the issues. Certainly the interactions with Jerry had felt good.

◆ ◆ ◆ ◆ ◆ ◆

THE FUNDAMENTAL

Balance

The Relationship Between Balance and Crisis

At some time during your life you will probably encounter circumstances so devastating that you will refer to them as a time of crisis. Personal and professional crises are a part of life. Our ability to respond with our essence and integrity intact is challenged by the nature of the emotions we experience when life goes out of control. The impact of crisis is the most common cause of imbalance.

A very familiar cause of the creation of personal and professional crisis which most of us can relate to is the downsizing of our largest organizations. The downsizing causes crisis for those who are left behind to do more with less. Those who have been out-placed as a result of the downsizing must reassess their entire career. Often they must cope with a job market as unforgiving as the companies they have left. Everyone is affected.

Few of us have been left untouched by professional crisis. If our crisis is not the extreme of an actual lay-off or loss of a job, we at least have a sense of frustration, hopelessness, or burnout from the demands of an unrelenting push for numbers.

Sometimes the crisis is more subtle. Professional crisis occurs one small step at a time, until one day you look around and wonder, "What am I doing here? I don't even like this. How do I know what is right for me?" At the same time, you find yourself fearful because you have no idea what else you would do. Or perhaps you do know, but the thought of what you would do is impractical due to your lifestyle.

The outcome of crisis, subtle or blatant, is the loss of balance. Do you know when you are off balance? Are you clear about how being off balance feels? Jerry was not. He was so absorbed with surviving that he was not even aware his decisions reflected symptoms of a man who had lost his balance.

The Paradox: the relationship between fear and balance

Imbalance is caused by crisis. Balance is achieved through crisis. Because the situation is severe enough to be a crisis, the events usually consume you. When you are consumed by a crisis, the situation amplifies your fears and your weaknesses.

Every step you take to fight your way back to equilibrium is a step you never take again. You are doing more than fighting the crisis. The crisis is only a crisis because of the fear. If you were not afraid, you would think of the situation as a problem, rather than a crisis.

You will find yourself living the same crisis again and again, possibly in a slightly different form. This reality is occurring because you are trying to teach yourself to let go of the fear. Perhaps you must recreate a similar crisis ten times before you are so worn out that you can no longer generate the energy it takes to stay in a state of fear. You remain in balance because you are too weary to maintain the tension to stay in crisis.

SYMPTOMS

How do you know when you are coping with a balance issue? Often events are moving so quickly you barely have enough time to respond, much less analyze yourself. Fortunately, there are symptoms.

Do you find yourself in a perpetual state of anxiety? Do others find you often awaiting the fall of the other shoe when things are good? Do you become intensely angry when others make a mistake making you look bad? Are you totally intolerant of mistakes in others?

Do you see ghosts? Are you the one who constantly prides yourself on always seeing the potential danger in every situation? Are you like Charlie Brown in the cartoons? At the drop of a hat, Charlie places his hands over his ears and laments, "We're doomed."

Are you afraid of failure? Do you contort yourself beyond reason to please others? Do you work endless hours on a relentless stream of tasks without feeling something is very wrong with your decisions to do so? Have you even examined the true necessity of each of these tasks? These may all be symptoms of a need to be perfect. The need to be perfect is dangerous when it is greater than your need to be relaxed and balanced. Perhaps another way of stating the same thing would be that your need *not* to be imperfect is driving you. Unfortunately, you are probably receiving reinforcement for your decision to self-destruct. It's cultural.

Other symptoms of a lack of balance include the urge to blame others and the environment and the economy and the competition for things gone wrong. Another symptom of balance issues is the large number of executives who move quickly from job to job, never staying long enough to be fully accountable for the many brilliant initiatives they create. They may be running from the potential of their initiative to fail.

Why are these symptomatic of a lack of balance? The examples listed represent a fear of mistakes or failure. A balanced person recognizes, comfortably, that inevitably things *will* slip through the cracks. Things will and do happen in spite of our best laid plans.

Burnout is another indication of a lack of balance. Burnout is a state preceded by an intense race to meet overwhelming demands for a very long time. You find yourself running harder and harder simply to cope. You have lost your balance long before you become aware you have burned out.

Burnout often comes from an inability to walk away and rediscover equilibrium. There is a certain amount of pride associated with the long hours and the scars of fatigue. In some ways to the wearer, the burnout becomes a badge of dedication. Instead, begin thinking of the inability to demand balance in your life as irresponsible.

121

Some symptoms of a lack of balance may be more subtle. You may experience a lack of vitality or energy or perhaps you find yourself quick to utter angry responses. Perhaps the symptom is a very real feeling you are not valued by the company. You may have a fear you are expendable.

Symptoms of a lack of balance may become severe. A serious symptom is despair. Everything becomes pointless. Why should you take the risks to do the right things when the whole system is working against the right action? You begin thinking about what else you could do at this point in your career. And the answers are not good. You have been trained to do what you know. You have a difficult time seeing alternatives. All of this leads to more hopelessness and resignation or desperation.

ASK YOURSELF

1. How well do you balance your need to work with your need for private time? Would your family agree with your answer?

2. How well do you know your own symptoms of a lack of balance? Are they evident to you?

3. Are you willing to take the risks to adjust your life when you are out of balance? Do you know how?

4. How often do you experience crisis? Is it often enough that you feel you are simply moving from one fire-fighting experience to another? If so, can you see that it is probably symptomatic of a larger problem?

LESSONS LEARNED BY POWERFUL PEOPLE

The causes of balance issues start early in life and become more severe over time. Often you will find childhood patterns establishing your lack of balance as an adult. You might relate to demanding parents who never seemed quite satisfied with your performance, even when you performed stunningly.

Competitive sports can also produce a professional lack of balance. Being compelled to be number one under all circumstances presents an almost insurmountable obstacle to well-balanced, relaxed adulthood. In fact, any part of your background where performance was valued over mental well-being is damaging.

Balance is a *way of thinking* about success and failure, winning and losing. We are born with potential, but we are taught how to think. If you really understand this concept, you have power to address things differently in your life. You learn to think differently.

A balanced leader makes mistakes and humbly accepts them as part of life. The balanced leader experiences business downturns with the same peacefulness with which he or she experiences the good times. Clearly this is not easy to achieve. You may even feel guilt at the thought of accepting failure with a sense of peacefulness.

As you evolve your leadership balance, you are tested again and again. Often the testing is what wears away your resistance to the impulse to throw yourself out of balance.

A. Know Your Hidden Needs

The resolution of balance problems often starts with understanding how you think about crisis. The crisis is the symptom balance is 'off'. Often leaders will repeat forms of the crisis many times without realizing they can change and therefore create a different outcome.

The key lies in understanding exactly what and how you are thinking when the crisis occurs. Do you really know what you are most afraid of around any given crisis? Do you know why you are so afraid? Do you realize the outcome you fear does *not* have to be the only outcome?

Make a conscious decision about what quality of life you want and what you are willing to risk to achieve what you want. Are you willing to stop making decisions based on fear? Are you willing to not be intimidated the first time you say "no" and you get put down? Are you fighting hard enough to demand that others respect your right to balance or is there a sense of defeat when you do not get a positive response?

Professional burnout or despair occurs as a sense of helplessness to change the outcome. We feel an impotence that robs our breath. The long hours and loss of personal time become imperative to getting the work done. If you do not finish the work, who else will?

What often stops us from saying "no" is our need for security and the fear of the power others hold over our security. We are sadly unwilling to take the risks affecting our personal lives or material needs. By not reacting strongly to important issues, you may ultimately be insuring a lack of security in your own future. The risk you are taking in not taking care of yourself may be far more serious than losing your immediate security. What are you sacrificing in terms of emotional and physical health, not to mention the relationships with your family that *must* suffer from lack of attention?

Action is your only recourse to professional crisis. To stay in an intolerable situation will only weaken your ability to fight over time. The trade-off you make to your own security will exact a price in the long-run which may not be worth the cost.

ASK YOURSELF

1. Think of your hidden needs as similar to the hidden codes on your computer screen. Often they distort what you are trying to do until you become aware of them. Do you have any needs that you can identify through careful observation that are keeping you in a state of crisis? For example, do you need to prove something to others? If you are in a situation where you can not win, do you stay with it because you have been taught that you should never quit? Are you sacrificing your balance because of a belief that is not serving you?

2. Make a list of trade-offs occurring in you life. Describe the quality of life you want, describe the life you have, and then identify the beliefs holding you in place.

MORE LESSONS LEARNED

B. How You Process

Suppose you are facing a disaster in your career or personal life (by your own definition of disaster). Understand what your mind does in such a situation. First, you have defined the predicament as a disaster. That is significant. Whatever has happened is, in your mind, being defined as an awful thing. Perhaps you have lost your job, or have been passed over for a promotion at a critical (your definition of critical) time in your career.

You are not just dealing with the event. You are also dealing with all of your fears around the event. All your worst nightmares become real, even before they have actually happened. You see yourself not being able to pay your bills, send your children to college, feed your family, etc. Whether these fears are real or not, you are drained by dealing with the fears before they are actually facts.

Not only do you see ghosts everywhere you turn, but your imagination will actually subconsciously take you even further down the road. Your panic will create a certainty in your mind of highly unlikely events. You may not realize the immobilizing fear you possess is of the level which occurs when you are facing immediate or certain death.

The intensity you may feel is because you have tied the event with your own definitions of failure. You may be experiencing as much pain from your sense of yourself as you are from loss of a job.

If you are experiencing a panic attack, ask yourself if the level of panic is commensurate with the worst-case outcome. Often your panic is much more intense than even the worst-case scenario would warrant. Your ability to identify the source of the pain is key to your ability to work your way through the crisis.

C. Perspective is Everything

During times of crisis, keeping a healthy perspective is critical. *Getting* to a healthy perspective is a matter of how you talk

126

to yourself. Identify what your fears are. Your fears provide a strong indication of your beliefs around what is happening to you. Once you understand what you believe about the events, you then can begin to reframe those beliefs.

For example, do you believe the loss of the job will disrupt your entire life in a negative way? Are you afraid losing your position represents a gigantic step backwards in your life process? Most people will automatically think you have stepped backwards. Differentiate what you feel from what you are afraid others will feel.

Pretend for a moment you had no fear about the loss of the job, but could believe instead the shift was a forced redirection of your life. Imagine the new direction will be a much more positive direction emerging as a result of the crisis. We would all like to be in control of those moves, but would you have had the courage to make a dramatic change without the force?

If you can direct your thoughts to the *freedom* the change gives you to create your life anew, rather than a sense of failure or loss, you will find yourself in a much better position to be the architect of a new future, for yourself and possibly your loved ones.

Viewing life-changing events as potential directions for a new approach to your profession puts you back in control. You can frame how you use the event to your advantage. The alternative is to become a victim to what is happening. Even a fear-inspiring boss puts you into a position of needing to evaluate your values and what you are willing to sacrifice to stay employed.

D. Controlling the Fear

Fear itself is the cause of most crisis. Fear has many symptoms. For some, it may occur as a vague feeling of uneasiness with a lack of clarity about the cause. You may find you awake in the middle of the night feeling as though you have forgotten something important. Other words describing the fear accompanying crisis are dread, anxiety, trepidation, disquiet, etc.

When you have conquered a fear, you react differently the next time a situation occurs which normally provokes the fear. You are calm and sure of yourself. You have been here before. You have survived. You have learned your lessons. You are very clear about what things you will say "no" to with your behaviors and your choices.

For example, perhaps your crisis was due to a bad boss. You turned yourself inside out to please and yet you were unable to please. The next time you encounter a bad boss, you react differently. Perhaps you spot the similarities sooner and do not take the job. Perhaps you do the whole cycle again. After running through the cycle enough times, you change fundamentally.

You begin to make the choices true to you because you have learned those are the only choices which do not perpetuate the crisis. You become calm in knowing life will always move in cycles and all you really have is your sense of self. There is no other security.

As you observe others, have you noticed a tendency for people to fall into the same type of problems repeatedly? Do you find it difficult to understand why they simply do not develop an understanding and avoid the same pitfalls? You may be doing the same.

Unless you intend to remain stagnant, you will continually change your circumstance to challenge your evolution. Ultimately, you seek a level of understanding which allows you to stay calm and focused in any circumstance. Balance is the most funda-mental challenge in your search for mastery of leadership.

The words you choose to describe your reaction to a crisis will depend on the depth of the crisis for you and the relativity to other events in your life. Your reaction to the crisis may have moments of terror about the direction your life is taking. Assume for now that these reactions all reflect a certain amount of anxiety that you can measure by becoming clear about the symptoms personal to you. Assume any response you have which is the antithesis to the way you feel in moments of peace, calm and tranquillity is a reflection of you reacting to a crisis.

Describe, as accurately as possible, the words that portray your state of fear. The next step is to attack the fear directly. Ask yourself what would make the fear be gone for good. What would have to be different for you to be unafraid?

The reasons for asking this question are twofold. First, asking this question helps you achieve more clarity about what you really fear. If the answer is "a certain amount of money will make the fear go away," you will realize your fear is about money rather than a lack of work. If the fear is a fear of failure, your reaction to the question of what will make the fear go away will be a vision of a highly successful, respected career position.

Each time you ask what will ease the fear, you will discover another level of what you need to do. This is the second reason for asking the question. Asking what would make the fear go away will help you clarify your next steps and what you want. If you are doing the exercise properly, your mind will give you an image of what your life looks like and feels like when there is no more fear.

When the picture is clear you should feel an immediate release of pressure internally. You will have a direction making you feel empowered until the next onset of symptoms. The next indications of fear tell you what you need to continue working your way through to overcome your fears. The fear becomes an ally. The anxiety will tell you when it is time to once again develop your vision further.

You will gain more and more clarity about your life. When you are on a path in tune with who you are and what your internal voices are telling you about what is good for you, you will find the fear recedes and is replaced with direction and clarity.

ASK YOURSELF

1. Identify your worst fear. Everyone has one or more specific fears for their future that are intrinsic to their personalities. What is yours? What would it feel like not to have that fear? Imagine circumstances so perfect that you no longer have the fear. What is different?

2. Now imagine that the fear actually comes true. Imagine ways that you would deal with the reality that actually free up your life in some significant way. Freedom is the key word.

MORE LESSONS LEARNED

E. Understanding Crisis As A Test

Balance is achieved through the tests the universe places in front of us. At times the tests may be so severe as to cause us to "quit". At these times the individual is truly separated from his or her ego. When things become difficult enough to cause the person to doubt himself or herself, it is a painful time of letting go of everything including the self-image the person may have built over the years. This crisis represents a time of powerlessness, and is humbling and challenging to the individual at his or her spiritual core.

When a person finally emerges from a test this severe, he or she must make a conscious decision to rejoin life. The dance is different forever. The leader will never be the same. He or she now understands how fragile life's balancing act really is. The person now realizes he or she has no real control. Hence the comment earlier in the chapter that the most evolved leaders approach success and failure with the same peacefulness.

If you are fortunate or unfortunate to be so tested, the basic humility you achieve will either end your quest for leadership or prepare you for the next stage of true power. The next stages of power C flexibility, impulsion, and collection C are only acquired through humility.

THINGS TO REMEMBER:

1. **Crisis is simply an amplification of your fears. If you were not afraid, you would not consider the situation to be a crisis.**

2. **In the midst of a crisis, do the unthinkable: Take time off to gain perspective. Examine your fear, and examine what would make the fear go away.**

3. **Determine what pattern the crisis represents in your life. See if you can assess what you are trying to teach yourself about where you have fear.**

CHAPTER IX

FLEXIBILITY

The word flexible indicates agility and an absence of rigidity and dogmatism. Flexibility *follows* the fundamental of balance because true flexibility occurs only when one is devoid of the aspects of ego producing arrogance. The same humbling process necessary to create the balanced person is necessary to develop the flexible person. Flexibility is built one moment at a time until the moment when you realize throughout your being you can not achieve your visions for the organization alone.

For some, this represents a spiritual awakening, often brought on by a period of intense personal or professional crisis. The key to whether the individual has learned balance is apparent in the way he or she interacts with others and with the environment. Balance issues force the person over time to recognize there is much that can not be controlled. The balanced and flexible person is able to let go of control and to understand decisions reached together are always better than decisions reached alone.

An individual has acquired a true state of flexibility when he or she has learned to respect *all* others for their contributions. Ultimately the individual's respect of others also indicates a deep respect and faith in the self.

John was holding a meeting in his office for his team prior to the large gathering with customers, suppliers, and employees scheduled for that afternoon. The meeting with John's team was scheduled for 9 a.m.

The meeting was starting late. Meetings at Sorot always started late. This time they were waiting for Debbie.

"She's never on time," complained Ned. "Why are we always waiting for her?"

AI think we're always waiting for somebody," suggested John. "Perhaps when we are late we don't think about how much time is wasted for all the other people."

"Sorry I'm late," said Debbie as she hurried into the room. "I was on the phone with one of the board members."

"Did you tell him you had a meeting to go to?" asked John curiously.

"Not really," said Debbie. "You know how those guys are."

"Given the state of crisis we're in, I'm going to suggest we don't have time to wait for each other, even when the caller is a board member on the other end," said John. "We need to get much better at just telling people we have made other commitments. I'm sure they will understand, and even if they don't, we don't have much to lose. Unless, of course, you consider the company."

"What do you mean?" asked Debbie defensively.

"We need every second we have available. It seems as if we believe everyone else's time is more valuable than what we have scheduled for ourselves. From now on, if you think the task is important enough to put in the calendar, it's important enough to stick to."

"Does that go for you, too?" asked Bob with a grin. "I mean if you call and want the numbers, and we're in the middle of something, do you want us to tell you to wait?"

"Absolutely," said John. "It also means we may need to be more careful of how we schedule our time. I think we need to ask if the appointment or the meeting is taking us closer to our view of what the organization needs. Our first need is to respect our own time enough to spend it productively. We all need to be much more assertive about our time. It's really all we have right now. If our time is being wasted, we need to say so."

"Well, I'm glad you're saying this," said Ned. "One of my pet peeves is getting to meetings and waiting for someone. If a person makes me wait I feel as though the person thinks his or her time is so much more important than mine."

"I said I was sorry," said Debbie in exasperation.

"I think we must realize everything we do is a symptom of right thinking or wrong thinking," said John. "In spite of what we believe, we didn't get into this mess by accident. When our suppliers, customers, or employees tell us they don't feel they're being treated with respect, you have to realize everything we do sends a message. I wonder how many times we've kept them waiting while we talked to a board member or someone else we considered more important? Let's all make a commitment right now we're all on time this afternoon for the meeting and then let's discipline ourselves better in the future."

Everyone nodded in agreement.

◆ ◆ ◆ ◆ ◆ ◆

THE FUNDAMENTAL

Flexibility

A person who has mastered the art of flexibility understands the organization is only as strong as the lowest common denominator. This individual appreciates each person's contribution or lack of contribution as critical to the overall success of the organization. He or she *never* assumes a superiority of one over the other, regardless of position or power.

When creating plans for change, the powerful person respects and values the input of everyone, even those who disagree fiercely with the view of the leader. The strong individual integrates the other person's opinion and resistance into the very fabric of the plan.

Flexibility is the true test of a person's creativity. In order to integrate the needs of those who have the most fear of change into an aggressive change program, the individual must exhibit openness and a willingness to examine the possibilities from a point of view that feels constraining. The concept of flexibility represents a sensitivity to others' needs even as the person is pursuing a personal vision.

Sensitivity to others' needs starts with the most basic elements of respect. Everything you do or say is evidence of your regard for others. Unfortunately, as you move ahead in positional leadership, you may take for granted privileges which are blatant examples of disrespect for others.

The first step to understanding the importance of a lack of respect for individuals in relationships is to understand the cost. The next step is to recognize some of the more subtle symptoms of a lack of respect within relationships in organizations. The third is to understand the cause.

One very visible example of the cost associated with a lack of respect within organizations is the cost associated with poor labor relations. Labor relations issues can be obvious or they can be very subtle. Immediately the mind leaps to bargaining and negotiation issues. However, anytime there is friction between people who work for and with each other, you have a labor relations problem.

Whenever you assume a person or a group of people are a means to achieve your goals, without appreciating your dependence on them, you are showing a lack of respect. Individuals or groups will often go to enormous lengths to show you how important they really are.

What is the cost of legal fees, not to mention the concessions which will be made during the negotiating process? How much of the anger and stubbornness stems from a sense of being a pawn who is considered of little value to the organization?

You may think you have been fair and just in your *actions*, but the real issue is what you *feel*. They will feel what you feel. If you believe they should be thankful they have the job with your company, you will find you communicate that belief. They will react in ways similar to how you react when you believe someone has demeaned or belittled *your* value.

There are other costs associated with indicating a lack of respect for others. Your suppliers will be quick to take advantage of someone who they believe is quick to take advantage of them. Your distributors will look for ways to "beat" the factory. Your customers will quickly identify any evidence of a lack of respect for their needs and rights. People within the organization will not pitch in and help when the task is outside their job description. They will be less likely to respond to urgency when we demand rather than ask. Your children will treat you with disrespect because they feel the disrespect coming from you.

ASK YOURSELF

1. List any relationships with the potential to make you vulnerable. Now list any relationships with the potential to make the organization vulnerable.

2. Do you view any of those relationships as a necessary evil?

3. Are there any individuals you believe are replaceable in your personal life or in your work?

4. Are there any people in your life who go out of their way to let you know they are important to you and that you would struggle without them? Perhaps they are responding to messages you are sending indicating they are not respected or valued by you.

SYMPTOMS

There are subtle, as well as obvious, clues telling you your organization is exhibiting disrespect to individuals or groups of people. If you are able to identify any of the following symptoms as being a part of your organizational reality, you may have a problem costing you *real* money. The obvious clues will be left to your imagination. The more elusive indicators will be addressed here.

For example, do people show up on time for meetings? Showing up late for a meeting shows a lack of respect for other people's time. Being late is an indicator you feel your time is more important than others'. If you are of higher rank or position, your lateness is perceived as a belief your rank entitles you to certain advantages. Being on time is an issue of basic courtesy and rank has *no* meaning. Those you abuse will begin to have less respect for

137

you because you have shown less respect for them.

Another indicator of a lack of respect for individuals is when clear, class-like distinctions exist among departments or groups. For example, do the sales people get more preferential treatment than other groups? Are there individuals or groups within your organization who feel their needs are less relevant than the needs of other groups?

Do pilots in an airline feel they are more important than maintenance, or flight attendants, or reservation clerks? Try to run an airline without all the parties. Try to run a business without *maintaining* an account once the client has been sold!

Until you recognize all individuals want to feel their contributions are vital, you will miss one of the biggest causes of lack of respect in organizations. You will subconsciously send messages indicating others are, in some way, less important than you are. If you or others are sending the message with regularity, you are creating potential problems for your future.

There are other subtle clues. Is there respect shown for other people's work load? Do individuals in your organization consistently ask others whether their plate is full before dumping assignments on them? Do people offer assistance when delivering assignments or is there an assumption the other person is there to serve? Do you or others indicate a false sense of urgency about assignments because you want yours to be addressed first? Do you hand your spouse a list of things to do as you walk out the door, without asking what they are trying to accomplish with their time?

If there is no vision for the relationships with internal support people, you are probably treating them as if they were a means to an end. They will, sooner or later, end up resenting your use of them to meet your own needs. Whenever they discover they are important only as a vehicle to get you where you want to go, they will begin to resist. If the perception exists for any period of time, you will find the resistance is accompanied by a surprising anger.

ASK YOURSELF

1. When you deliver assignments to others, do you always ask if they have the time? Do you care if they have the time?

2. Do you find yourself thinking an individual or a group of employees should feel grateful for their jobs? Do you feel your family members should be grateful to you for all that you do for them?

3. Are some meetings or appointments acceptable for you to be late? If so, are you more conscious of being on time for your boss than for your subordinates? Are you more conscious of being on time for work related issues than you are for your family. If so, do you understand the message you are sending them about the importance of *their* time or about their importance to you?

4. Do you make commitments and not keep them?

LESSONS LEARNED BY POWERFUL PEOPLE

There are many reasons for all of the subtle ways individuals feel and *show* a lack of respect for others. If you want to understand whether you are being disrespectful of others, start by examining your belief systems. You may believe certain kinds of education, background, or jobs are more valuable than others.

You may, for example, assume the more preparation for a job, the more respect the person deserves. You forget, when you operate on this assumption, everyone has been somewhere during the time some people are acquiring an education. There are people you work with who may have learned some very difficult life lessons while others were in school. Every human is invaluable and each has an important part to play. Whenever you put others above you, or yourself above others, you show your lack of understanding of the interdependence we all have.

Are there any subtle judgments you hold about how hard you worked to attain a certain status or position? A truck plant in Indiana years ago held many surprises for a consulting group brought in to work with teams in the labor force. In the plant there were many highly educated people including a Ph.D. in economics, a world class chess champion, and many individuals holding advanced degrees.

It is also important to look at *what* you judge as superior. Is education more important than wisdom, for example? In the coal mines you will often find a greater degree of wisdom than in many other professions. There is an interesting maturing process occurring with people who live in dangerous professions. They are often more intuitive and more sensitive than you might expect.

Another cause for subtle disrespect can be attributed to our need to judge others. If someone does things less perfectly than you would do them, you may immediately form a conclusion about the person affecting your response to him or her. You perpetuate a cycle that invites others to judge your own lack of perfection.

We tend to treat others as we are treated. If people dump on you without asking, you will not think twice about dumping on others. The behavior of dumping becomes expected. If you are expected to never say you have had enough, you will probably expect others to do the same.

You often show a lack of respect for yourself when you do not honor commitments. When you believe you can not tell certain people you already have an obligation on your schedule, you are indicating your choice to place the commitment on your calendar was misguided. Those who must await you have become victims to your inability to say no to those you view as superior. This could be a boss or a client or anyone else who you are allowing to intimidate your sense of self-worth.

If using and abusing people is part of our work ethic, we need to ask why we exist. If quality of life is one of the costs of our pursuit of success, than what is the success expected to bring us?

THE STORY

John and the group worked through the morning. They were under a tight time frame to prepare for the afternoon's meeting. There were many issues.

John wanted to rewrite all their agreements with the suppliers. Jerry, who was rather subdued today, did not agree. He felt the loss of face the organization would go through would be traumatic.

"You know," Debbie said, "I think I know why this solution is so elusive to us."

"Why?" asked John, concerned they would never be ready to present a united front at the meeting with the suppliers, customers, and labor leaders that afternoon.

"Because you are trying to make the decision in a vacuum," she replied. "You have no idea what the suppliers really want. Before you make a decision that you have treated them badly and you need to give away the shop in order to get their support, you might want to see what they feel. Even if you could reach a conclusion, you might find they refuse to accept your conclusion."

"I see what you mean," said John. "It makes me wonder if our whole approach to this meeting isn't wrong."

"Why? What are you thinking," asked Bob, who was getting particularly nervous about the meeting.

"Because we are putting ourselves through hoops trying to come up with answers before the meeting so we can present them. I'm wondering if we haven't gotten off track from our original intent. We started out pulling all these people together so we could listen to them and here we are planning to tell them what we will do again."

"Perhaps we do because we feel safer," said Jerry quietly. "Maybe we feel too scared to go in there and ask them what they want. We might not want to give whatever they might ask us to do."

Everyone looked at Jerry in surprise. He seemed different somehow today; less attacking and less defensive. Something had happened to him.

"What ideas do you have?" asked John. "I'm a little lost."

"Well, let's say we are afraid, and with good reason. We haven't built any trust with these guys. I'm not sure fear is such a bad thing. Fear makes a person cautious. When you let the fear control you into doing the wrong things, you're making a mistake. At least I've been letting my fear make me too controlling. That has worked against us. I found myself defending every decision without being open to whether I was right or not.

"I'm thinking," he continued, "our best path might be to tell them exactly what's on our mind; what we're thinking and what our constraints are. And then let them offer suggestions. But we make it clear we are simply looking for choices."

"What if we don't like their choices?" asked Ned. "We need to be very careful we don't dig ourselves into something we can't dig out of."

"We are already dug in," said Debbie in annoyance. "You always want to take the risk-free road, and we can't afford that right now. We have everything to lose by not moving."

"I think we might want to incorporate what Ned's saying into our approach," said John. "He has a point, and any ground we lose is dangerous.

"Look," John continued, "We have to figure out just how to integrate what everyone wants into what we want. Each of us will have our own agendas and mistrusts going into the room today. Even if we disagree with anything someone says, we will need to find a way to work through the issue. If we don't, we will never get the whole team together."

"I really don't see how we can," said Ned. "It's just too risky."

Jerry cleared his throat. "I think I'm beginning to see what John means," he said. Everyone looked at him. "We have been fighting among ourselves forever. If I say it's white, Debbie says it's black, and vice versa. Look at where the fighting over control has gotten us. We are stuck with no way out. What if every time someone says something we disagree with, we try to integrate his or her idea into our idea. I wonder where trying to cooperate might take us.

"For example," he went on, "if I think Ned is being too cautious, and I simply tell him so, I've gone nowhere. If I follow John's suggestion, and assume Ned may have a point, I try to work out a more cautious approach he can live with still getting me where I want to go."

"Why are you coming at this so differently?" asked Debbie with real curiosity. "I think I'm beginning to like you."

"I did some real soul-searching," said Jerry. "I had no idea how rigid and controlling I had become. John had to show me my behavior in a mirror. I also realized nothing in my life was 'working'. If things had been working, I doubt I would have heard what he said to me. But when I looked at the mess we had created, and all of our opinionated battles, I realized if I wanted to get anywhere, I was going to have to learn to give. I could be 'right' forever, but so what? I guess, before, I was afraid giving-in meant I was saying I had been wrong. That was just too hard to do."

"Well then," asked John, "how are we going to handle this meeting? We need to exhibit the same kind of flexibility Jerry is discussing and protect ourselves from the obvious dangers. What do you suggest?"

Ned said thoughtfully, "I guess our biggest danger is pricing ourselves too low, or agreeing with labor on things which undermine our position for the future. Not to mention paying our suppliers too much and running our costs up even higher. If we can solve the problems without undermining our position for the future, I guess I could relax. Perhaps we just need to tell them what we need. If they can respond, great. If not, we're really no worse off than we are now."

Bob Skipper, having sat silently to this point, entered the conversation. "This is the first time I ever remember this group actually trying to work through something, rather than everyone taking a stand. I wonder if we could use some of what we've learned to break through the barriers of the group this afternoon? Asking the right questions, and understanding where and why they are resisting, is key to our forward movement. We've been so caught up in our own beliefs and needs and we've never really tried to incorporate, or integrate the needs of our customers and our employees. We always end up in defensive positions. We say things like 'I hear what you're saying, but....'."

"Why do you think we've had such a hard time getting together?" asked Jerry with genuine curiosity. "I have my own theories, but I'd like to hear yours."

"I'm not sure I'm wise enough to understand all the reasons," Bob responded. "But I do think there are a few obvious things we can learn from. First, we all seem to be afraid cooperating is compromising our integrity or something. Second, we seem to hate any idea that isn't our own. We need to get over that. Third, we act as though every issue is a personal arena for us to forward our own career. We gain some ground and we are not about to lose the ground, even if what we have accomplished is not for the good of the whole. I've been as bad as anybody."

"Interesting," said John. "What do we do next?"

"I think we're doing what we need to," said Bob. "Frankly, we started when you walked into the board meeting and made a game out of getting them to help. You immediately started turning a hostile situation into a group effort by asking everybody to help solve the problem. I've seen dramatic changes in your leadership style over the last few weeks and the new approach is making a big difference in each of us."

"What are you seeing?" asked John.

"I'm seeing someone who is not making decisions from fear anymore. You've hit your stride. You also seem to have gotten much more involved in truly understanding the problems at the deepest level. I can't speak for everyone, but I have more confidence when you operate from a sense of what you are trying to create personally rather than what you think you 'should' be doing."

"It has been interesting, added Debbie. I've seen the same things, but I've also noticed you avert some of our conflict by simply asking us how we would build on each other's ideas rather than letting us fight over who's right. The change is subtle, but I've been a lot less angry and a lot less scared.

Ned chimed in. You know, the last couple of weeks you've actually been listening to me, too. As the legal guy, I think companies often think of me as a necessary evil. I always feel as if I have to fight just to protect the company and I haven't felt like the company valued my view. Today when you suggested trying to find a way to follow the course of action you wanted and make me happy, all the steam went out of me. I found myself wanting to cooperate."

"I'm not sure where we are," said Jerry, "but I feel a lot more hopeful. If there are answers, we'll find them."

"Well, let's all take this attitude into our meeting this afternoon, and see where a new perspective takes us. It has to be better than where we are," said John.

◆ ◆ ◆ ◆ ◆ ◆

MORE LESSONS LEARNED

People resist change. All change must be built on the understanding people need to balance their need for personal security against a focus on doing the right thing.

Understanding and working *with* human nature is critical in helping people to make necessary adjustments when confronted with change. The truly flexible leader understands this and works with the desires and motives of others to accomplish results.

A. Elitism

Many of our leaders skilled in strategic, analytical thinking know only too well the cost of not understanding the human factor. Brilliant restructuring or new alliances often do not come close to reaching their potential, due to the complexity of dealing with the human emotions involved. The difficulties General Motors experienced in the acquisition of Ross Perot's company, EDS, is an example. Many of the people involved will testify that the differences in culture and personalities had a major impact on making the transition very troublesome. Many years passed before a level of trust was established allowing the two companies to work effectively together.

The General Motors' systems people were threatened because they worried about their job security. Many of the EDS employees were operating from the belief General Motors' systems were outdated. This led the GM people to feel EDS was arrogant. These and many other attitudes created enormous transition problems. The leadership of both companies questioned publicly the quality of the partnership.

To increase the odds of a successful transition in major structural or cultural changes in organizations, you must comprehend and respond to the reasons why people facing change will sometimes sabotage their futures.

We may have to look closely at our own processes for dealing with change to understand. People are very adept at playing certain kinds of games to adjust their perception of reality. They will view themselves as successful and wise when they are not. They will believe in their own capacity to always pick the best path when they have a history of foolish choices. They simply adjust their reality to fit their view.

Even if they have been vocal critics of their situations in the past, they will often believe their current situation is better than a suggested or forced change. They have to! Otherwise, these individuals resisting the change would have to admit they lacked the courage to leave their job for a better situation.

Think of this resistance to forced change as a form of elitism. Our nature is to want to be smarter or better than others. (Remember, we are trained to be competitive.) When you are operating at your wisest, you are more likely to be humble or admit you do not know everything. You understand there is much to learn and others may, in fact, possess ideas you have never conceived.

Unfortunately, when we feel threatened, as we often do in times of change, we tend to fall back on our instincts. We like to believe our way is better, others do not understand our particular situation, they're naive, etc. We feel better about a situation over which we have no control if we believe their knowledge or understanding of the circumstances may be less than ours. In the case of organizational change, often we are put in a position where a new system, process, or organizational structure will be imposed upon us against our will.

How often is your reaction to become defensive about how well you were doing *before* they came along? Suddenly, the things you were upset about before the transition are lost in your need to defend your brilliance.

A natural coping mechanism is to believe we are smarter or more knowledgeable than those who would come in and do our jobs "better". This need to feel smarter is functioning at a subconscious level. The individuals are unaware of the need as a factor in their behavior choices. The resulting behavior is often stubborn and argumentative in nature.

In the case of General Motors, many of the GM systems people believed the EDS people simply did not understand GM's business as well as they did. They resisted many of the changes EDS tried to implement, even though the methods had been tried successfully in many organizations. If there was a problem with an implementation, the reaction of the internal GM employees was one of contempt for these outsiders who thought they knew better.

When one of EDS's key executives traveled directly to as many manufacturing locations as possible, things began to change. His agenda was to problem-solve with plant managers and GM employees. Feeling as though they were being listened to, as opposed to being treated as inferior, was part of healing the relationship.

B. Choice

A *second* key factor in understanding the resistance to change is the importance of *choice* as a cherished right. People want to believe they have choice in things having a major impact on their lives. When reality intrudes, human beings will still find a way to execute a sense of choice through their actions.

Often, if all other choice is eliminated as an option, we will find ways to sabotage success in order to have a choice. That our actions are self-destructive becomes irrelevant. Our children will do the same, and it is probable that as a teenager, you did the same.

C. Sense of Self-Worth

Another important factor in managing major transitions is the influence of people's beliefs about their worth. Many of us have learned to expect and demand a great deal from our bosses, our employers, and even our country. Rather than thinking in terms of what is good for our companies or our country, we think in terms of "what's in it for us" in most situations. We *appear* to have created a nation of people who operate from a sense of entitlement.

The psychology of what is happening is actually more complex than pure selfishness. Once you have acquired something, you will operate from a sense of having earned your right to keep the rewards of your labor. The reward becomes part of who you are and your sense of your total value. You do not think in terms of un-earning things. The word does not even exist. Therefore, when you are asked to give something up, your sense of self-worth is being violated. Self-worth is the issue when individuals refuse to give up something which is clearly counter-productive to the long-term goals of the whole.

As a nation, we are in a state of great change. We are attempting to create needed transformations in our businesses and government. Many of the changes may be critical to our continued well-being. Many of the commentaries on what is necessary to reverse the negative trends in our society and industrial world call for *sacrifice*. Unfortunately, this is the very framing of the problem ensuring the change is unlikely to occur.

Whatever you are trying to accomplish, you must find a way to frame the changes that is *not* perceived as a sacrifice or a loss. You must find ways to make the necessary changes as a part of a natural flow, rather than a painful intervention. A frequent saying of a well-known German horse trainer is "Make the right things easy and the wrong things difficult."

Work with an understanding of human nature to be successful. Human beings will cling determinedly to the wrong path if a change violates their sense of elitism, choice, or self-worth.

ASK YOURSELF

1. Are you aware that the majority of people believe they look five years younger than they are? Do you believe you look five years younger than your actual age?

2. Do you believe yourself to be at the cutting edge of your

profession? Is your organization at the cutting edge?

3. If your organization were to implement a new system for managing data, how much resistance do you think you might get from those who believe the current system is adequate? How many arguments do you believe you might hear indicating that the current system is somehow better?

4. If you were asked to completely change your software on your own system to upgrade to newer, more technologically advanced software, how open would you be? What arguments are forming now as you think about the reality of such a change?

MORE LESSONS LEARNED

Overcoming the realities of why you and those you would like to influence resist change demands a great deal of creativity and flexibility. There are certain changes people *do* welcome. For example, if the change improves a sense of *elitism, choice, or self-worth*, individuals and organizations will be more likely to welcome change and work in a positive direction.

You can work with techniques to help adjust people's belief systems about rewards. If you are tuned to the real issues behind the resistance and asking the right questions, the adjustment is not always difficult. You will, however, need to exercise a great deal of discipline and attention to detail.

You cannot assume participants in your change effort will necessarily see the positive impact of the change. This is especially true if they are facing any sort of perceived loss. You must act as a facilitator of the change to help them view the impact on their lives differently.

Rather than acting as an information giver or as an order giver, your role is defined as one of facilitator. The leader makes the change easier and simpler for the person who perceives himself to be the "victim" of the change. By asking the people affected to think about what this change could mean in terms of an improvement in their situation, you are helping them to frame a way of looking at the issues. Rather than dwelling on the negatives, you are helping them to look for the positives *or* a way of turning a negative into a positive. This is a very different response than "telling" people all of the good things coming from the change.

In creating a new or stronger alliance, to ask those affected to offer ideas and suggestions for ways to create an even greater sense of elitism is a strategic move. *You* may believe the change will enhance their position or their opportunities, but do not assume *they* believe what you believe. Offer them the opportunity to build the vision for the new alliance with you and you may find, together, you create a vision greater than yours. This process is equally important when asking a family or any organization for that matter, to welcome change.

Remember, if they had no *choice* in the decision to make the change, they are very likely not thinking about the change in the same manner as you are. They may see the transformation as a loss or a step back personally.

If new structures to support the change are not yet clarified, people may be more worried about what is coming than focused on making the change work. The last thing they may be thinking about is how much better the organization will be because of the change.

Focusing on the *psychology* of the impact of change on the people involved makes managing change much more complex.

You are not simply responsible for looking strategically at where your organization must go next. You must also consider the impact of what you are doing on productivity and moral.

Giving attention to maximizing the people potential during the transition will improve the outcome. What was good simply becomes better. Remembering you, too, are probably affected by your own sense of elitism, self-worth, and the need for choice will probably help you to remain sensitive to the needs of those you influence.

ASK YOURSELF

1. If you are attempting to create change and meeting with resistance, what do you think you could learn from those resisting the change? Might they already know some things you need to know? If so, what?

2. Are you guilty of arrogance when asking others to change? What could you do to test yourself?

THINGS TO REMEMBER:

1. **The psychological elements affecting you and others are probably related to your sense of elitism, choice, or selfworth.**

2. **The solution to changing the responses of others or yourself to more positive reactions are within your understanding of the psychology.**

3. **If you are experiencing a lack of cooperation and respect from others, examine whether you are showing others a lack of respect.**

4. Your flexibility is directly related to your ability to manage your own arrogance. Always ask yourself how to build your ideas into the ideas of others rather than attempting to implement your ideas at the expense of others' ideas.

CHAPTER X

IMPULSION

Impulsion exemplifies the person's ability to gather together all available resources and knowledge to create the desired outcome. To attain the maximum impulsion on any initiative, the leader must understand the issue of commitment. Commitment is the deepest form of engagement.

Commitment is an intense dedication to an outcome allowing no external interference. Commitment also represents the individual's passion and belief in self. If you know yourself, you become more effective at building commitment in others. From commitment comes impulsion.

♦ ♦ ♦ ♦ ♦ ♦

THE STORY

John was on his way out of the building to get some lunch. As he walked to the parking lot, he saw Larry, the local union president, walking in front of him.
"Larry, can I talk to you a minute?" John called.
"Sure, what's up?" Larry responded.
"I'd like to brief you on what we are thinking about the meeting this afternoon and get your advice," said John.
"Sure. I'm really looking forward to it. You guys sure know how to set yourselves up as targets," said Larry with a big grin.
"Well, that's exactly why I wanted to talk to you," said John. "You're as aware as anyone of the financial difficul-

ties we're having?"

"Oh no you don't. You're not going to get any commitments from me before the meeting so you'll have an easier time. You get exactly what you deserve and I'm not going to bail any of you out. If you had paid attention to what we've been telling you for years, you wouldn't be in this mess."

"Actually I had something else in mind," said John mysteriously.

"What?" asked Larry, a little surprised by John's lack of defensiveness.

"I want you to make the meeting especially tough on us. I want you to come at us with all of your guns loaded. I want you to tell us and our clients every mistake we've made in the last three years. I was afraid you might go easy on us because we're in front of all our clients."

"What's your game?" asked Larry suspiciously. "You never cared what we thought before."

"To be honest, I need every employee's commitment if we're going to save this company for any of us. The only way I know how to get commitment is to build the future together. Unless we all examine what we want and are not getting from this company, we'll never get there. If the management is not willing to expose itself in order to change this organization together, I doubt you will ever trust us. We don't have time. So I want you to take us apart in front of everyone."

"So we'll believe you?" asked Larry.

"So you'll know we're willing to take risks and so you'll know we're serious."

"You are serious!" Larry said with surprise. "I thought this was just another one of your opportunities to stand in front of all of us and tell us how you had the situation in hand. None of us would have bought that, I can tell you."

"We know we don't have the answers. We also all agree we have not really tapped into the work force to figure out the right course of action. We ask for concessions, we tell you how bad the situation is, and then we don't do anything to fix the problem. We've got to do this together, and we need your help."

"It may be too late," said Larry. "My troops are pretty mad that you let this thing get as bad as it has."

"Frankly, Larry, we all got here together. We've all been asking what the company can do for us, without realizing we needed to protect Sorot for the future. I'm sure you see a lot of selfishness on our part, but perhaps we've all been thinking more about ourselves than what's good for the whole thing. If you really think about it, some of the things you ask for would be plain foolish for the company. I'd like us all to think more about what we would do if this really were a company we had bought together."

"So what do you want from us?" asked Larry again.

"I want total honesty, I want all your complaints, and I want an attitude acknowledging we need to figure the solutions out together. I want an openness to solving the problems rather than winning. We need to let go of blame and really work on fixing the problems."

"And what do we get back for all of this openness?"

"You need to decide what you want. We can continue fighting over this item or that item on our negotiations, but the fighting isn't getting us anywhere. Unless you consider continually undermining our future getting somewhere, that is. We have to decide we want to work for a healthy thriving company and then we have to understand what that means. Until we do, we may keep fighting over the wrong things."

"I don't agree with you we're fighting over the wrong things. If we don't fight for the weakest guy on our side, no one else will, and you guys will take whatever advantage of him you can. We have to fight for benefits and job security."

"I think there's a different way to look at this," said

John. "Suppose management began to understand, really understand, being fair and rewarding people is the only way to keep people from feeling the need to fight just to be respected and valued. And suppose we all finally 'get it' that job security only happens one way."

"What do you mean?" asked Larry.

"Isn't job security your most important issue?" asked John.

"Of course it is," said Larry emphatically. "But there has to be a quality of life to go along with security as well. Having a job is not the only thing our people worry about."

"Well, the only way I know to guarantee any sense of job security for any of us is to create a healthy, thriving company. That's all our responsibility. I don't see us getting there unless we're all moving in the same direction. All the concessions and promises we make during negotiations are only buying time. If the company continues to flounder, there is no such thing as job security, no matter what you get from us in the negotiation."

"So what's your point?" asked Larry.

"My point is we need to do this together. We need to get honest, even if being honest doesn't feel good, both ways, about the kinds of things we're fighting for that are destroying this company. We need to take a good look at what we know and decide what we are going to do next. But we will never get off the ground if we continue fighting each other. We may move forward, but there won't be enough impulsion to save us."

"I'll think about it," said Larry. "I need to talk to the union before the meeting, and get their reaction to all of this. I'm not sure whether they aren't mad enough to sink the ship because they think you deserve to suffer the way you make them suffer."

"Obviously, they have the power to do that. But what do you really win if you do?"

"Maybe the people in the fancy offices making the bad decisions will finally understand you need us. And you need us to do more than routine, meaningless stuff. Some of the things you ask us to do are such a waste of time!" said Larry.

"Maybe. But maybe we are understanding our flaws now. We're asking you to tell us all those things today and in the future. Look, Larry, we have all made decisions bringing us to this spot. The question is, can we start making decisions which will bring us out of this and allow us to enjoy our work and each other at the same time."

"That's a pretty tall order," Larry said skeptically.

"I guess it is," said John. AI happen to believe it's possible. And I don't much like the alternatives!"

John and Larry walked away from each other, each immersed in their own thoughts. Jerry, who had watched the entire interaction from the door of the building, smiled and said quietly to himself, "That son of a gun might just pull this off."

◆ ◆ ◆ ◆ ◆ ◆

THE FUNDAMENTAL

Impulsion

Think of impulsion as the forward momentum and force a person is able to achieve through his or her actions and choices. The actions and choices are the impulse or signal creating the momentum.

The ultimate and ideal form of impulse to create organizational or personal change is commitment. Imagine an organization with 100% personal commitment from each and every employee.

Clearly, most of our organizations operate somewhere shy of such an ideal.

What would be different? Think about the crusaders you have known. Nothing stops them. No task is too great. It is hard to imagine them saying, "That's really not my job" if some obstacle were to appear in their path.

The antithesis is an organization full of individuals with no zest for their work. The lack of commitment translates into a lethargy and a lack of taking full responsibility for outcomes. Lack of ability to make a commitment can even become a cultural attitude of ostrich-like behavior, with no one looking out for the well-being of the whole and everyone worried about getting their share before the resources are gone.

So where do you begin if you would like to create an organization full of people who have a personal commitment to the health and wealth of the organization as an entity? You must first start with you!

SYMPTOMS

Unfortunately, identifying results as a lack of commitment is difficult. The lack of true commitment shows up as a number of other ills that are, in themselves, large problems. If the majority of us are lacking in the fundamental quality of commitment, how do we recognize the problem in ourselves, much less in others?

Organizational structures provide mythical boundaries to results. Job titles and "areas of responsibility" become the excuse used for not taking responsibility for outcomes. You must ask yourself how often you become stuck while waiting for someone else to make a decision or take action. Waiting for someone to give you permission to complete things is a symptom of missing commitment. When the commitment is solid, somehow everything gets done in spite of who has the positional authority. When commitment is not solid, the result is a lack of impulsion.

Other symptoms fall into familiar examples. Lethargy and world-weariness are prevalent symptoms for many people. Vitality and passion are missing for the work. Feeling overwhelmed by the amount that needs to be done also is a symptom of lack of commitment.

The key to recognizing the symptoms to a lack of commitment, and therefore a lack of impulsion and momentum, is to realize when you are truly committed, nothing stops you. Instead of feeling overwhelmed, you feel exhilarated. Anything less than total, exuberant participation indicates a lack of commitment.

LESSONS LEARNED BY POWERFUL PEOPLE

According to Webster, to be committed is to "be responsible for." What leaders are trying to create in organizations at every level is a sense of personal responsibility for the outcome. Creating this sense of responsibility in others is a difficult and complex task. You must first identify your own level of commitment to the work you are doing.

You are looking for a benchmark against which to test yourself. By creating some symbol for your own commitment, you will be able to question yourself moment-to-moment to see if you are operating at your most powerful. Often our favorite sports offer an appropriate symbol.

For example, some people think of the strength and follow-through of their tennis swing as an appropriate symbol. They compare their current activity level around some work-related objective by representing the activity level with an imaginary tennis swing. The tennis swing that materializes will either be powerful or something less. The individual's mind will never lie. If a person is approaching the work in a less than totally committed manner, the image of the mental tennis swing will be less than all-powerful.

Create the image of your swing in your mind and ask yourself if your current level of activity and intensity would equate to your most powerful swing. Perhaps you play golf or racquetball. By asking yourself to create a mental image reflective of a symbol like a tennis swing, you can check yourself and get a very clear picture about how you are operating around some key issue. You do not need to actually play the sport. The swing is symbolic. What matters is that you place in your mind an image of your most powerful swing as if you were playing the sport in the most powerful manner. Then create an image of you now as if your work represented your swing.

What if you find through your imaging that you are not operating symbolically in your most powerful swing? Perhaps you do not swing all the way through. What does that tell you? Your image is clearly telling you that you are not totally focused and therefore not totally committed to whatever you are doing.

Why not? That is the question you will want to answer for yourself. Often the problem with the swing in your mind is related to a lack of clear purpose in what you are working on.

ASK YOURSELF

1. Are you operating at a total commitment level? This is not a question of how hard you are working. It is a question of commitment

2. How frequently do you complain about the lack of per-

sonal responsibility in your organization or in other family members? Is it possible you are dealing with a lack of commitment? If so, can you identify any reasons people might not be totally committed?

MORE LESSONS LEARNED

A. Diagnosing the Problem

A lack of clarity regarding purpose or meaning in life will often create the kind of lethargy or lackluster performance most of us see too often. Victor Frankel's book, *Man's Search for Meaning,* focuses on this issue. In his observations of concentration camp inmates during World War II, he found the loss of meaning in people's lives had a direct impact on their survivability.

The 'meaning' we are addressing goes beyond the sense of personal direction discussed in Chapter VII. To cultivate commitment in yourself and others, not only do you need to understand who you are and what you contribute, but you need to identify purpose and meaning in everything you do. You must not allow anyone to waste your energy or your time attending useless meetings and performing worthless tasks.

Not only does a lack of purpose affect your vitality, not having a clear purpose affects satisfaction in your work as well. You may find the absence of purpose also influences the way you interact in your personal relationships. At times when you find the symptoms of total commitment are lacking, a good place to start looking for cause is within your own sense of personal purpose or vision.

Are some of the assignments lacking in meaning? Could they be a reflection of someone else's insecurity? Do you sometimes give others assignments that lack meaning?

B. Overcoming Obstacles to Personal Commitment

It *takes* commitment to build commitment in your life. That is the paradox. Dedicate yourself to finding a way to live your essence through even the mundane things you do. If you tennis swing follows through best at those times when you are doing things reflecting your essence, you must decide how you will deal with the times when the meaning is not there.

The next step in building commitment in the organization is to understand the impact you have on others. The fundamental of flexibility becomes key. Until John began to realize he needed to listen to and truly understand the viewpoints of those with whom he disagreed, he did not have a chance of getting through their defenses.

As a leader develops an understanding of personal meaning and an ability to incorporate the needs and essences of others into the task, he or she creates a foundation for developing commitment, and therefore impulsion, for the organization or the personal relationships he or she values.

The key to getting Larry committed to turning around the organization was understanding the union's issue was job security. Larry needed to see meaning in the actions, as opposed to more empty gestures. The leader must recognize tasks having no meaning are tasks diverting energy from the essence of the leader as well as others.

Are you prepared to stop asking people to do meaningless tasks? For example, asking sales people to fill out time logs to account for how they spend their time often creates great resentment. Ask yourself what you are trying to accomplish in terms of monitoring work performance and looking for discipline in the sales force, and ask if there is another, less demeaning, way to get there.

As you apply the process of creating a purpose and a meaning to everything you do, you will find you are better at dealing with irrelevant tasks thrown at you. The answer always lies in clarity.

If you know what is bothering you about the task, identify what need someone is trying to fill by the task, and look for other ways to fill the need. If the need seems irrelevant to you, ask yourself what you are going to do about allowing someone to rob you of the meaning of your efforts.

ASK YOURSELF

1. Consider all the tasks your employees or family members are asked to do. Identify any tasks they do that do not help move the 'organization' forward or keep the organization out of legal trouble.

2. Are you prepared to remove all meaningless tasks from their responsibilities?

3. Are you performing meaningless tasks? Are you committed to them? What are you willing to do to remove them from your responsibilities? If you do not take risks to remove them, what is the alternative risk to your vitality? Is it worth it?

THINGS TO REMEMBER:

1. **Check the image of your performance against an image of your tennis swing often. If you are not swinging all the way through in your mind, see if you can**

discover why.

2. Determine whether you are totally committed to the work you are doing now. What would you need to make you committed if you are not? How can you incorporate more purpose into what you are doing?

3. Be sure each thing you ask others to do has meaning and is not based on fear.

CHAPTER XI

COLLECTION

Collection is the final, basic fundamental for developing a person's leadership capacity and personal power. Collection reflects the individual's understanding of oneness with the others on the team. A leader must also reflect a oneness with the entire ecosystem. Leadership is no longer as simple as leading others to greatness. If you are truly involved, you must lose yourself in acting for the greater good of the whole.

THE STORY

People began arriving early for the meeting. Jackie ushered them into the company auditorium where they were holding the session. She found their expressions and mannerisms on arrival indicative of the attitude they would bring to the discussions.

Some of the customers looked impatient and annoyed. "Probably think this is a waste of their time," thought Jackie to herself.

The suppliers all looked a little anxious. "They have as much riding on this as we do," she thought with surprise. Jackie had not previously comprehended that the problems of the Sorot Corporation were probably creating the same kinds of crises in the lives of the suppliers.

Some of the union leaders looked relaxed and expectant, while others looked like they were spoiling for a fight.

Jackie began to feel sorry for John and his team.

John looked relaxed and cheerful. Jackie was glad. He was more like his old self these days and she had every confidence he could do anything. Jerry looked thoughtful, while Debbie, Ned, and Bob all looked nervous and almost a little frightened.

As John began the meeting, everyone was alert and curious about what would happen. For everyone in the room, the meeting was unprecedented. There had been union/management meetings before, there had been supplier meetings, and certainly the customers had been asked for their opinions. But never had they all been asked to attend a meeting of a company in trouble. Including all of them would simply have been too volatile and dangerous. There were so many ways the gathering could backfire. Too many pieces of laundry might get aired in front of the wrong audience. Everyone wondered how the CEO could possibly look so relaxed.

"I suspect, at times, this meeting will become uncomfortable for some of us," John suggested, voicing all of their thoughts aloud. "The issues we face are serious and that creates a high degree of emotion. I want you all to understand why I felt we needed to do this together, even with all of the very apparent potential land mines.

"No matter how much we might want to detach ourselves from this crisis, we will all be affected by the outcome of what happens to the Sorot Corporation. Some of us, clearly, have more to lose, or gain for that matter, than others. But the people represented in this room form a system. Each of us makes our livelihood by interacting with the others. If you remove any element from the room, all of us will be affected. Even those of you who are customers and are looking at me a little skeptically right now, will feel some pain on some level, if Sorot ceases to exist.

"You may think you would just find another supplier and

your lives would go on. But the entire system would be affected. Perhaps without us as competitors in the composition of the industry, your prices would rise a little. Or there would be an impact on the quality of our competitors, who no longer have to view us as someone to consider in the market place. If our suppliers are affected, the impact on their business might affect the ability to get parts to our competitors in some way. All of us are part of a larger whole, and we will never be able to predict what dominoes might fall if any of us disappeared."

John was calm and confident in front of the group. So far he had not said anything to touch any particular nerves, so the audience was still in sync with him. Some people even had thoughtful looks on their faces, as though they had never thought of themselves in the context of the larger system impacted by each other.

"Because we are part of the whole, I'd like to frame this meeting and our agenda in an unusual way. We asked you here because we want your input. We know we are struggling. We know we aren't making our customers happy. We know everyone who works at Sorot doesn't feel he or she has always been treated fairly. And we know our suppliers have thought of us as ruthless and unconcerned about their realities as we've struggled to survive.

"We know all that, and we open this meeting with our heartfelt apologies for being so short-sighted in our selfish quest for success. And the bottom line is our selfishness has not helped us to be more successful. For that, we are also sorry. No company starts with a vision of failure. No person would knowingly create a reality like we have created for ourselves. We're not only struggling at an organizational level to understand what went wrong, but many of us are also struggling at a personal level to comprehend our own accountability.

"We have no intention of making light of any of those

personal accountabilities. But, we'd like to ask all of you, as you give us input that may help us to 'right' this ship, to stay accountable, as we go through this process, to the larger vision of making us all successful. If we can fix the problems together, we all stand to win. If we spend all of our time in blame, we may walk out of here with less than we had to start. I'd really hate to see that happen for all our sakes."

Larry raised his hand and, as John acknowledged him, everyone held their breath. They all knew how contentious the union had been recently and the leadership team in particular braced for the onslaught.

Larry surprised everyone. "As the spokesperson for the union, I'd like to make a statement about our accountability and our hopes for this meeting," he suggested.

"Please," said John.

"We've had some intense discussions about our future and this company," said Larry. "Even before this meeting was announced, we were forming some interesting conclusions. We had pretty much decided we had very little to gain by seeing this company go out of business. We've been mad at what we believed to be mismanagement of our future, and yet, we've come to realize our taking the company under to prove we were right began to seem more and more foolish. We've also seen a big difference in attitude from management over the last few weeks. They've been listening for a change. We want everyone here to know we're standing behind management, and we're willing to do everything we can do to help solve the problems, as long as the solution doesn't blatantly work against the good of our membership. We, as a group, are choosing to define the good of our membership as things also good for the company."

John was grinning from ear to ear. Others had expressions of amazement.

Leslie, the CEO of Sorot's largest single customer, stood. As the group turned to acknowledge her, she began to speak. "Sorot has supplied us with parts for years. The last several years have been rough, to say the least, and we've diverted a lot of business to other suppliers in the last six months. Quality has been terrible and the delivery issues have been a nightmare. We were prepared to pull all of our business over the next six months as we built relationships with other suppliers."

Several on John's leadership team groaned. If their largest customer canceled, Sorot would be out of business.

Leslie continued. "I'm not so sure anymore. I wish my team had the guts I see in this room. I don't know what you are going to do to solve these problems, but I've seen a lot and I guess I believe enough in the human spirit to believe you can do anything you set your mind to. When a group takes the risks you are, and makes itself open to the help of everyone else, the company will be successful. I'm willing to continue on our current contract for a while if you let a couple of our engineers come live here for a while to help. If things improve, we'll gradually increase our orders to you over time."

Jerry and Bob looked at each other in amazement. The first cannon had not even been fired and they were already getting the support of the most important players in the equation. How did this happen?

"Besides," Leslie continued with amusement, "none of the other manufacturers seem to be doing much better. I think the disease Sorot has is catching. You may just be onto the cure and I, for one, would like to take advantage."

John stood and spoke. "We're really grateful, Larry and Leslie. I promise we will do everything we know to honor your commitment to us. I feel as though I have a whole new lease on life. Here's what we are suggesting for the rest of the meeting. We need to know the worst side of everything that has happened. We're asking you to sit down as groups C customers, suppliers, labor C and tell us all of the things you think have contributed to our problems and particularly our relationship problems with each of you. Then what we would like to do is mix the groups and have the mixed groups help us decide how to fix things. We think this way we'll get some ideas and you'll all have a chance to vent some of the frustrations building over the last few years."

"What guarantees do we have you'll follow our advice?" asked one of the union committeemen.

"I can't guarantee anything until I know what you are recommending," said John. "But I believe if we all look for solutions benefiting the whole, as well as Sorot, we'll find ways to implement your ideas. The challenge for all of us is to be honest about how we feel and work to find the solutions that make us all feel good. We're going to have to respect each other's positions even as we attempt to solve the problems. We have to stop looking at things from our own point of view all the time. I absolutely promise we will either buy into your ideas or attempt to integrate them somehow into the final solutions."

The groups divided up and began the task of fixing the Sorot Corporation's problems.

◆ ◆ ◆ ◆ ◆ ◆

THE FUNDAMENTAL

Collection

Collection, as a fundamental of leadership, demands the leader pull together the visions and needs of the entire team. The team, by definition here, will not just include the immediate members of your own team, but all of the players within the ecosystem. By definition, the concept is all-embracing. Your view must become larger and larger as your awareness grows. While the other roles and fundamentals are demanding, the ability to view oneself as part of a greater whole calls for the utmost sacrifice. Learning collection is to learn to sacrifice the ego.

The leader must develop a greater understanding of the dynamics of the group's interactions. Only through this understanding can an individual continue to evolve to the highest levels of mastery, both as a participant of groups and as a leader. Only through this understanding does the organization have a future, for the destiny of the organization is a collection of the destinies of the individuals.

Leaders are asked to embrace many visions. There is their own personal vision, combined with the organizational vision, whether it be a company or a family, in conjunction with the personal, individual visions of the others who the leader influences. To balance and honor all of these visions is the true function of the master.

SYMPTOMS

Symptoms of a lack of collection show up in the turf battles occurring in every organization. If you find yourself fighting for resources for your segment of the organization without considering the tradeoffs that must be made by others for you to have your way, you are probably missing *collection* in your understanding.

Most organizations continually witness fights for resources between marketing and sales, sales and manufacturing, finance and everybody, etc. Generally this means the department heads are doing a good job on their responsibility to manage down, but a lousy job on their ability to see the needs of the collective whole. Families surface similar issues as one member attempts to influence the direction of the whole, often with little thought for the impact on others. Where else do we learn our self-centeredness?

Divisions should look out for other divisions. Instead they compete. Competition within an organization is usually destructive. At the very least, it represents energy no longer available to compete against outsiders. Strong leaders also recognize destructive win or lose competition with anyone in the ecosystem, including competitive businesses, often leads to disaster. Win or lose sets up a potential you may not want to embrace: losing.

Another symptom of an organization or leader with problems with collection is indicated by the relationships with suppliers, distributors, community, etc. Are you concerned with the welfare of your suppliers or distributors? Do you see them as a part of your responsibility? You will know if you or your organization have developed this quality by the quality of the relationships. If your relationships with your suppliers are focused on cost-cutting and constant negative negotiations over the same issues, you have a problem. If your distributors have a love-hate relationship with you, ask yourself if you are looking out for their interests as well as your own.

There is always a price to pay for an imbalance in the ecosystem. We often learn the lessons of collection through crisis. A person we love suffers from addictions, mental or physical. When you trace the issues, often you will find a person who has sacrificed, willingly or unconsciously, personal well-being for others in the group.

Stronger members take advantage of weaker members with little concern for the consequences of the weaker members. It may take years before the imbalance becomes apparent. A spouse goes through a mid-life crisis and rejects the entire family. The family system was not working for the individual and he or she did not know how to demand more balance before precipitating a crisis. The wise and powerful individual senses and attempts to adjust the imbalance long before a crisis emerges. Crisis is a mechanisms to re-establish balance in any system.

At the level of business an example might be the US auto industry. The industry treated dealers badly for years. Dealers were a means to an end for the manufacturer. Besides they were making lots of money. It became personal. When the industry had a problem, the solution was often to pass the problem to the dealer. The dealers rebelled and created the opening for foreign car manufacturers and the rest is history.

Community is also an important part of the ecosystem. Northwest Airlines went through enormous community relations problems at a time when they were trying to enlist the aid of the community for funding growth opportunities. They began to find how critical the relationship was to their future.

These stories are not uncommon. Collection is an imperative part of the growth of the individual desiring to be the master of his or her universe. The sooner a leader learns to accept responsibility for the health of the entire ecosystem, the better his or her long-term state of being.

LESSONS LEARNED BY POWERFUL PEOPLE

When any individual or leader focuses his or her choices too tightly on personal or isolated group incentives, the loss is enormous. In doing so, the leader has forgotten the lessons learned in his or her own growth. The need to help *all* participants achieve their vision is only developed after a leader understands how important personal vision is to his or her own motivation.

There is a bit of magic that enables an individual to respect all visions simultaneously. The individual visions and essences of the participants in the leader's world will all blend together in a harmonious whole. Because the essence of the individual always reflects some core value this person holds in honor, those values speak to the essence in all of us. For example, if one person's essence is teacher, another will be student, or learner. There is an observable balance of essences within any ecosystem which, if utilized properly, becomes a powerhouse for creating and implementing ideas.

If a person asks for and probes the essences and the personal visions of those who interact with him or her, he or she will often find those essences have all of the ingredients needed to create any reality. The challenge for the leader is to not be intimidated by structure and job descriptions or influenced by traditional roles and responsibilities, such as male dominated family structures. A powerful leader can be found in wise children who often understand more than jaded adults.

By identifying the essence of individuals and groups, the leader allows the most enchanted structures to emerge through the chaos of our current structures and organizational charts.

The balance may not be apparent in the current job structures or descriptions or traditions. You may find a history of bad relationships with suppliers. You may be led to assume balance is attained by keeping suppliers and others under control.

Perhaps your best nurturers are nowhere near the customer service function. Your most direct, honest communicators may not have access to the leader who needs to stay engaged with reality. The teachers may be in a position of perpetual "do-bee" because they have a history of being efficient. *And* you will often find people who have deep core values to contribute are very unhappy because they are not allowed to do so.

ASK YOURSELF

1. If you were to strip your organization of job titles or traditional role responsibilities, and simply made a list of individual essences, what complimentary qualities begin to emerge? Would you be comfortable having your title or position stripped? Would you know where to focus your energy?

2. Are you considered a wise leader by your subordinates? Would your peers consider you a good leader? Do they trust you and your judgment implicitly?

3. When confronted with a battle for resources, do you look out for the other's needs with as much intensity as you do your own or your organization's? Do you know their situation, constraints, limitations on resources as well as you do your own?

MORE LESSONS LEARNED

Often the chaos in your organization is a result of the ecosystem attempting to right itself. The turf battles generally lead to restructuring, first centralizing and then decentralizing as the organization struggles to regain balance.

The pendulum swings from one side to the other as organizational "karma" attempts to normalize the laws of cause and effect. In the business world, issues with suppliers become a problem over time. Labor becomes a problem over time. Everything off-balance is affected by everything else. Unfortunately, as organizations crisis-manage their problems, the universe may be thrown more off balance by decisions meant to solve a specific problem.

The most important role you can play as a leader in such an environment is to take ownership for everything which is not working. This ownership extends beyond the immediate areas of accountability. Your ownership expands to include the whole universe of your organization.

If you are fighting with suppliers, do not even bother to sort out and correct the problem until you understand the entirety of their relationship with their universe. If you have a labor problem, understand the political nightmare within which labor leaders live. They must please their constituency but they must also survive. They often walk a tightrope. What is good for the immediate concerns of their constituents might set a precedent leaving them politically vulnerable. Your issues may not be their priorities.

If you need to cut your costs and you do so at the expense of your suppliers, how will your decision affect their ability to give you the quality you need? You may assume their competition will step in and supply what you need, but this is a long-term strategy for disaster; another lesson from the auto industry.

As you identify your career needs, do you consider the needs of your family? Are you being fair to them? You may be the breadwinner, but if you view that as a right to affect everyone's reality in a negative way as you pursue your goals, have you thought about the consequences? Are you clear about the overall vision you have for your family or are you consumed with a personal vision for power and position? Does power and position become more important than healthy well-adjusted children? If so, you will ultimately pay the price for your focus.

THINGS TO REMEMBER:

1. **Mastery assumes a responsibility for the whole. In a crisis you will find remembering that you own the**

178

responsibility for the good of the whole difficult. To abdicate responsibility is to admit you are *not* a leader.

2. Real leaders are responsible for the long-term as well as the short-term outcomes of their decisions.

3. If you are experiencing a problem within your area of influence, examine all of your relationships to determine what the essence of the problem is.

4. Identify the personal essence for each participant and determine a way to utilize the essences to create the outcome you desire. Remember, the outcome should be a feeling, not a specific goal that benefits you.

IN SUMMARY...

SUMMARY

Clearly, John's team is far from finished. They have only begun the process of fixing the problems. But they have developed an understanding of their responsibilities as leaders and individuals. They are realizing the implications of fear-based reactions and the danger of operating selfishly within a system. At the individual level they are each struggling with their own accountability. Sorot is an organization of people that is beginning to step up to the challenges of leadership at the most fundamental levels. In volume 2 of *What To Do When It Rains*, John's team must begin the process of healing the organization as they have already begun the process of healing themselves.

John and his team are maturing in their concepts of individual responsibility. As John develops his capacity to operate with rhythm and balance, as he engages more fully with his environment, as he develops his own sense of direction, his team grows with him. His process allows them the room to grow. He asks what is important of them rather than what is expedient. As he does so, they are freed to be more effective. To free people to be effective is a form of magic.

We place so much ownership for the success of an organization on the leaders because of this phenomenon of transference. We have recognized for some time that the leader determines the organizational personality to a great extent. Unfortunately, we seem to focus on the output of leadership rather than the process. The process is where the healing occurs.

The last chapter in this text provides an overview of the entire sequence of fundamental elements of leadership and personal mastery.

182

CHAPTER XII

OVERVIEW OF THE MODEL

You are an experienced human being. You're good at what you do. You have a history of making good decisions and you possess a certain amount of confidence that you're just a little smarter or a little quicker than average. You're also experienced enough to be a little humble. Sometimes, being confident and good at what you do is not enough. The old rules do not seem to apply.

To solve any crisis, there is always a starting point. The three phases, and the fundamentals following each phase, offer a process for discovering the root issues in your decision-making dilemmas.

Each step toward harmonizing diverse visions is a step toward a larger realization of harmony within the ecosystem. There is a maturing process demonstrated by development of the ten fundamentals. Each step in the sequence integrates a larger view of the whole.

The first phase focuses on the internal mechanics used by the individual to make decisions. You learn to recognize the importance of relaxation, rhythm, and freedom as elements affecting how you address fear. As you incorporate these understandings into your development, you become more free to focus around you.

In the second phase of development, you begin to manage the confusion debilitating many people. You focus outward and try to make sense of the environment and your role and responsibility in the environment. The act of doing so mandates a clarity about your own personal sense of direction and purpose. This prepares you for the last phase.

In Phase III, you take the external focus further. You become responsible for maintaining balance and understanding through the worst of circumstance. You become a truly powerful person. You are no longer just paying attention and reacting. You are now accountable for the inclusion of others into your thinking and planning. To make the leap into Phase III in your development, you go through cycles demanding again and again that you lose the negative, insecure aspects of your ego. You are learning to manage personal power by managing an aspect of your personality and the personalities of those you interact with: arrogance!

The last stage of letting go of ego is collection. In collection you become *one* with the entire universe. Your universe may simply be the collective universe of your particular organization. If you choose, the universe becomes even larger. The more evolved you are, the more responsibility you absorb.

Each step in the process of creating strong and flexible human being builds the foundation for the next step. You will never exert your maximum power if all of the steps are not firmly in place. As you read through the overview of the model that is the essence of this text, imagine you are assessing yourself against each of the qualities outlined in the present moment. After you have read the entire text, simply turn to the chapter you need in times of crisis.

Phase I: Preparation

Managing Fear

In the first phase of exploring your evolution, you examine your ability to stay calm and make decisions in difficult circumstances. Each of the three topics covered within Phase I (Relaxation, Rhythm, Freedom) represent an aspect of your ability to handle risk. If you are lacking in any of the fundamentals in Phase I, you will be unable to make good decisions in adverse circumstances. Or the missing ingredient may mean the difference between good decisions and great decisions.

RELAXATION **RHYTHM** **FREEDOM**

Relaxation: If you are stressed, tense, or fearful, the tension will affect the quality of all your decisions. If your objective is to evolve as a truly wise person, the very first step is an absolute. There *must* be a focus on your ability to detach from tension De taching is the most basic of steps.

Rhythm: Rhythm, in the context of developing yourself, is the quality of being even and measured in the response to all situations. Your pacing is consistent. You do not rush or move too slowly. This quality will be impossible to attain if you do not achieve mastery of the previous fundamental, relaxation.

Rhythm is a reflection of your ability to handle risk. If your timing or pace in decision-making is erratic, you will need to pay particular attention to your responses to risk.

Freedom: Freedom is your ability to base actions and decisions on the 'right' thing to do in the given moment. You must make decisions without the need to please others.

These first three fundamentals represent a relearning of your sovereignty. We all lose some of our sense of self as we become more responsive to the expectations of others. Your ability to take risks is drilled out of you as a child and often as a young adult to some degree. Often, over time, the addition of responsibility closes down the very things making you most effective. The retraining of the basics must occur within the framework of the responsibility you bear as an adult. Can you reestablish your natural state of relaxation and freedom and rhythm within the frame of the responsibilities you now carry?

Phase II: Consistency

Managing Confusion

This phase represents your ability to lead others. Phase I creates a basis for decision-making. Phase II reflects your relationship with your environment. If you are lacking in any of the fundamentals in Phase II (Engagement, Responsiveness, and Direction), the missing quality will be reflected in the people relationships and the trust issues you encounter.

The next three fundamentals flow directly from the first three and actually establish the strength and control necessary to build consistency in leadership style.

ENGAGEMENT   RESPONSIVENESS   DIRECTION

Engagement:

The next basic quality is an ability to be immersed in the environment. You have a great awareness of what is happening around you *and* the interplay that occurs with each event. To be powerful you cannot remove yourself from reality. In the evolution of the effective individual, engagement *follows* relaxation, rhythm, and free dom for a reason. Good news and bad news are sought equally without fear. Are those you interact with comfortable bringing you bad news?

Responsiveness:

The next step is responsiveness to the reality discovered in engagement. Your ability to adjust to surroundings quickly is not the same as rushing. If you have fully developed the fundamentals of relaxation and rhythm, your decision-making looks and feels fluid and smooth as opposed to rushed.

The foundation for responsiveness is built through the previous fundamentals. As a responsive person, you should be relaxed, involved, and make thoughtful, fearless decisions moment-to-moment based on a clear view of reality. If the fundamentals are not in place, responsiveness appears as a 'catch up' or 'fire stomping' mode.

Your responsiveness is a direct reflection of your ability to pay attention and respond to the laws of cause and effect. If your decisions are often challenged or if decisions lead from one crisis into another, you are not responding to the right input or at the right time. Perhaps the information you have gathered (i.e., the way you are engaged) is not accurate or clear or in some way your ability to process risks is being affected by some force.

Direction:

You must begin to develop a deeper sense of self or direction. To determine a sense of direction, you must have a clear sense of personal strength and purpose. If you respond to the environment without having a clear sense of personal purpose or direction, you will create confusion for yourself and for those attempting to follow you. The essence for this sense of direction lies within the essence of you. If you have not yet discovered your own inborn sense of direction, or mission, you must seek understanding and coordinate what you learn with reality. This becomes your benchmark for all decisions.

Note: One of the most important outcomes or by-products of this phase is trust. Only when you have created a consistency in your responses do people learn to trust you. You can not achieve this trust without being able to describe your essence and how your essence fits within everything you do.

Phase III: Power

Managing Arrogance

In Phase III you will determine your ability to create and influence change. The sections in this topic (Balance, Flexibility, Impulsion, and Collection), offer a unique and important stage of evolution of the truly powerful individual. Symptoms of missing elements are an inability to motivate and influence others to achieve concrete results.

The last set of basics develop the finesse a person needs

to be truly extraordinary. When complete, they create a picture of contained and disciplined power. There is a sense of control without being controlling, of power without rigidity. There is no sense of chaos or depletion, but one of cat-like readiness and flexibility.

BALANCE FLEXIBILITY IMPULSION COLLECTION

Balance:

Balance is represented by your ability to be centered or stable in the face of great stress. Your balance develops as a result of being tested over time. The balanced individual exhibits a great awareness of the cycles of change. You have reached the maturity necessary to find a comfort in knowing there is an ebb and flow to all things. When thrown off by an unexpected turn, you quickly and yet not erratically are able to reorganize.

Flexibility:

No reality is created *alone*. The influence and input of others is what makes the strength of any outcome. If you are flexible, you stay balanced in a sense of personal purpose, but are able to adapt information available in the fears and fantasies of others into your decisions. You do not judge. There is no bitterness or blame, but instead a constant building or developing. When things go wrong, you assume this is part of the fabric and look for ways to use the crisis for leverage. A flexible person is similar to a bird building a nest who finds a use for everything. Nothing and no one is discarded as irrelevant.

Impulsion:

You become a catalyst for the growth of others. By valuing all input, by showing the use of the input through demonstration, and by weaving the information into a mosaic more powerful than any you might have created alone, you act as a motivating factor to move reality. You free the energy often stuck as people resist each other and each other's ideas.

If you have developed impulsion, you have integrated your vision with all the resources actually available to you. As a result, you are able to unleash the force of each person's potential as well as your own. This is not possible when you are not balanced in your own ego responses to others or in your need to please.

Collection:

In this step, you should be able to gather all personal power and launch at any target with momentum and grace. The intrinsic quality or attitude allowing this to happen is a deep understanding of the connection of all things.

Collection comes from a state of relaxation, personal vision, and a balance of other qualities outlined in this text. If you are the only one who knows the answers, or if you believe others represent interference to your brilliance, you will never reach your full potential. This concept represents one of the greatest challenges for gifted people. One of the qualities of the gifted person is often a belief in self. This model assumes this belief in self will never be enough to reach true greatness. In the collected person's world, there is no management/labor division; there is only the whole. There are no suppliers or customers. There are no caste systems. In this person's world, there is only one ecosystem where each part is integral to the whole and all is functioning in harmony.

There are many levels of development within each of the basics outlined above. You might achieve relaxation with a job and your responsibilities, and then you fall apart when you lose a job or do not get a promotion. How does one maintain a sense of rhythm when confronted with such adversity?

Use and reuse the fundamentals in the text to discover where you may need to focus your self-exploration. Each crisis demands from each of us an integration of the fundamentals. By identifying the weakness set off by the specific crisis you are in, you will discover the reason why you needed the crisis. This weakness defines where you must next evolve!

EVENT	SYMPTOMS	CAUSES	RESOLUTION	MAN-AGING
Relaxation	•constricted breating •muscle soreness •tension in others •quick to despair	•fear •destructive beliefs •instinctive reaction to situation •lack of balance in lifestyle	•concentrate on breathing •practice muscle relaxation •balance lifestyle isolate and reframe damaging beliefs	F E A R
Rythm	•rework •inability to make decisions •procrasti-nation •impatience •lethargy	•low tolerance for risk •inability to evaluate risk effectively •lack of courage •lack of personal self-confidence	•examine worst case scenario •create vision for desired outcome and path to it •don't fight reality •anticipate the patterns •identify positive outcomes from mistakes	F E A R
Freedom	•lack of flexibility •lack of innovation •impossible schedules •victim mentality	•poor judgement •history of bad outcomes •fear •worrying abut what others will think	•develop intuition •develop plan with imput from others to diminish risk •identify causes for insequrity	F E A R

EVENT	SYMPTOMS	CAUSES	RESOLUTION	MAN-AGING
Engagement	•fear of bad news •struggles to maintain status quo •lack of awareness of organization •inability to deal with reality effectively	•concept of scarcity vs. abundance •survival mentality •need for personal security	•nothing to lose mentality •bold choices •express curiosity about *everything*	C O N F U S I O N
Responsive	•insensitivity •repetitive crisis	•lack of accountability •victim mentality	•determine cause and effect relationships	C O N F U S I O N
Direction	•personal crisis •lack of trust by others •confusion in others	•no personal vision •personal vision confused with personal goals •lack of freedom (reliance on other people's opinions	•identify connection between your personal vision and the crisis •manifest personal essence in solving the crisis •identify and leverage the essence of others	C O N F U S I O N

EVENT	SYMPTOMS	CAUSES	RESOLUTION	MAN-AGING
Balance	•victim mentality •loss of perspective •hate your work but lack resolve to change it •see the downside of everything •feeling out of control •intense fear of failure	•crisis •fear •rigidity •control issues •imbalance in personal life •lack of seasoning	•understand your hidden needs •disengage from the crisis •monitor your self-talk •identify what will ease the fear •identify why you have created the crisis and what it is teaching you	A R R O G A N C E
Flexibility	•arrogance •standoffs with others regarding best path •reputation for stubborn-ness •sabotage of your initiatives •lack of success with foolproof initiatives •experience others as arrogant	•lack of respect for contribution of others •seeing others as inferior •lack of understand-ing of inter-dependence	•identify whether you or others are operating from elitism, self-worth, or the need for choice •pay more attention to the the psychology of change and less to your view of the desired outcome •manage your own arrogance	A R R O G A N C E

194

EVENT	SYMPTOMS	CAUSES	RESOLUTION	MAN-AGING
Impulsion	•inability to create a good team •lack of commitment •lack of follow-through	•meaningless work •lack of respect for visions of individual team members •motivating through fear	•check personal commitment to to initiative •if you are not committed, do expect others to be committed •do not assign meaningless tasks because of personal fear •find a way to reframe initiative in a manner you can commit to	A R R O G A N C E
Collection	•self-serving attitude •single-minded devotion to your own outcomes at the expense of others •inability to make decisions for the good of the whole at your own expense •poor relationships with others outside	•career focus as opposed to focusing on quality of life •internal reward system based on material gain or advancement •lack of vision •sense of protecting subordinates at the expense of others	•take respons-ibility for the health and well-being of the whole •take ownership for *everything* that is not working •examine the ripple effect of all your choices	A R R O G A N C E

immediate area of responsibility while maintaining good relationships with subordinates

195